RED, WHITE & BLUE-COLLAR

A Common Man's View on an
Un-Common Country

Jonathan E. Gibson

WestBow
PRESS
A DIVISION OF THOMAS NELSON

ISBN: 978-1-4497-5984-1 (sc)
ISBN: 978-1-4497-5983-4 (hc)
ISBN: 978-1-4497-5985-8 (e)

WestBow Press books may be ordered through booksellers or by contacting:

WestBow Press
A Division of Thomas Nelson
1663 Liberty Drive
Bloomington, IN 47403
www.westbowpress.com
1-(866) 928-1240

New York City
© Anthony Furgison | Dreamstime.com

Library of Congress Control Number: 2012912677

Printed in the United States of America

WestBow Press rev. date: 09/13/2012

WE THE PEOPLE *of the United States, in Order to form a more perfect Union, establish Justice, insure domestic Tranquility, provide for the common defence, promote the general Welfare, and secure the Blessings of Liberty to ourselves and our Posterity, do ordain and establish this Constitution for the United States of America.*

-The Constitution of the United States, 1787

CONTENTS

Introduction

REALITY CHECK

Have you ever wanted to make a difference and do something for the betterment of America, but didn't know what to do or where to start? Have you ever really wanted to do something, but then stopped because you convinced yourself you couldn't or it wouldn't matter anyway? Have you ever looked back on your life and felt regret because you knew you could have made better personal choices and led a more satisfying life that could have made a difference to others and your country? I'm sure many of you reading this would answer yes to the above questions; I know I do. I have looked back at my life and have seen a lot of wasted time. Not only have I seen where I wasted time and life, I have also come to my own conclusion that I am tired of just living and not doing something to help my fellow Americans and my country. Fortunate and rare are the few who can say they truly have no regrets and their lives display what America is all about.

My life has been a blue-collar life. For over twenty years, I have held a job where day in and day out, there's nothing but physical labor. I know many of you can relate. It hasn't been my first choice, but there is dignity and pride in being a blue-collar worker. In all reality, blue-collar workers built this country and still build and maintain it. Without us, we wouldn't have roads and houses or the conveniences of fast-food drive-through windows and grocery stores. We wouldn't be able to get our plumbing fixed or our trash picked up. The things we generally take for granted involve doing things most of us wouldn't want or choose to do, but someone has to. That someone is a blue-collar worker.

Unfortunately, it seems Washington DC has forgotten the common man and the important role he plays. The common man I'm referring to is every man and every woman who does the thankless, often low-paying, dirty, sweaty jobs that make America run. That is probably the majority of American workers. The common man is the individual who demonstrates daily silent heroism while trying to provide food, clothing, and shelter for a family. The common man is the average, everyday person not seeking fame or fortune, but who just wants the peace of mind that comes from knowing he or she has the right to life, liberty, and the pursuit of happiness. Sadly, over the past few years, this peace of mind and right seems to be slowly disappearing, causing despair and oppression for most Americans.

By writing this book, I am trying to encourage, inspire, and remind any and all who read it that this is still America, and anything we set our minds to is possible. Through pointing out a few things we all know to be wrong and offering a few simple suggestions on how to make them right, my main intent is to stir your heart and help you realize we can and must exercise our rights as American citizens to change the course of our country. If we can do that, we will regain our respect, our dignity, and our total sovereignty and freedom. I am including a few extra things so you won't just be reading my opinion, but also some things that will remind you or make you aware of what America was founded on and what America stands for.

I know you may not agree with me and my views on all of the topics in this book, and that's okay; I just hope you read through it and get a reminder or even a first-time realization of the fact that we aren't a hopeless, helpless people. We are the most blessed and powerful nation to ever exist, and we need to start acting like it. Just because America is here today doesn't mean it will be here tomorrow. Complacent for too long now, we have taken for granted what we have, and, by doing so, we are carelessly allowing our freedom to slip through our fingers. It is time for us to wake up and realize this country belongs to us, its citizens, and not to the handful of people we elect to govern it. They work for us, and they need to be reminded of that. If not, and if we don't wake up right now and realize what's going on around us, when we do wake up, it will be too late and everything that we've worked so hard to build and maintain will all be gone.

I hope you enjoy what you read, and I hope you are inspired as a fellow American so we can stand together in unity and with one voice proclaim, "One nation under God, indivisible, with liberty and justice for all."

Chapter 1

RESPONSIBILITY

Pledge of Allegiance

"I pledge allegiance to the flag of the United States of America, and to the republic for which it stands, one nation under God, indivisible, with liberty and justice for all."

America: one seemingly simple name, one seemingly simple word, yet how profound it has been in shaping the history of mankind yesterday, today, and hopefully for centuries to come. For just a little over two hundred years, we have been the hope of the world in the constant fight for that one simple, basic, inalienable right: freedom. The road bringing us to where we are today has not been an easy one, nor will it ever be. From the beginning, countless lives have been lost and countless, selfless sacrifices made. The road has been paved by both men and women, by people of all colors and creeds. The road has been paved by people who could see beyond themselves and look at a bigger picture. They knew what America meant to them and could see what it would mean to us and the world in the future. They saw and knew the promise of America.

Today, every day, those same selfless sacrifices continue to be made by men and women of every color, faith, and background. The sacrifices continue to be made by those who can see beyond themselves and seek to secure America for tomorrow, just as our Forefathers did for us. With the ever-growing anti-American, anti-God, anti-everything-we-stand-for sentiment around the world, now more than ever it is paramount that we, as a nation, stand together as Americans—not black, not white, not yellow, red, or whatever other color you can think of, but Americans. We must, and I emphasize *must*, open our hearts and minds to what is going on around us in the world and unite under the banner of the stars and stripes. We absolutely *must* stand together as one nation under God. For the sake of our country and our children, we have no other choice if America is to survive. At the very least, we need to live as a nation in a manner that honors all those who have given of themselves in the past and present, so that their sacrifices were not in vain.

As a nation, we need to reflect upon where we have come from so we can decide where we are going. We must look at our mistakes so we do not make them again. We must look at our triumphs to learn what we did right so we may continue to triumph. We must reflect, we must remember, and we absolutely must stay vigilant. In today's world, one mistake can literally cost us our country and our freedom.

I believe before our nation as a whole can reflect, decide, and move forward, we, its individual citizens, must do so first. We must honestly look into our heart of hearts and see where we stand, because we are America. We have inherited the greatest nation to ever exist on the face of the earth. We have been handed the responsibility of continuing and passing on the gift of freedom and the pursuit of happiness to tomorrow. The duty is now ours.

Today's world is much different than it was decades ago. There are different morals and standards. There are different thoughts and feelings about honor, respect, and duty. One of the more disturbing trends is the thought that being an American is a right, not a privilege. Just because most of us are born here doesn't make being an American a right. I believe a lot of people have lost sight of that. We are the beneficiaries of sacrifice from generations before us.

What it means to be an American is slowly being lost. It's not being taught in schools or homes anymore. In some cases, teaching about the very essence of our foundation is now illegal. Ever increasingly, we hear about how prayer and certain words of the Pledge of Allegiance and our national anthem are offensive. It's no wonder that America is slowly being lost.

I understand we all have rights as Americans regarding freedom of speech and religion. I believe most of us understand that. However, it's practically treason to omit and illegalize the very principles and beliefs that helped found this country to begin with. Even if one doesn't agree with some of the founding beliefs, primarily God and prayer, at the very least those beliefs should be respected enough to allow their continued teaching. It is because of those founding beliefs that one can disagree to begin with, without fear of being jailed or put to death. It is because of those founding beliefs that one can even call oneself an American.

However, even though one may live here, if the beliefs that founded this great nation and made it strong are too unbearable and unthinkable, then perhaps he or she needs to leave. There are plenty of other countries that don't share our beliefs. Go there! No one is forcing anyone to stay here. That's the beauty of this country: you're *free* to go! Go elsewhere and trade places with someone who will cherish this great land. Make space for those who really know and understand what we have here. Allow those who love this country to become productive citizens here while you go elsewhere. That may sound harsh, but that is how I feel, and, I dare say, that's the general consensus. As the saying goes, "If you don't love it, leave it."

Granted, we do have a lot to work on here. There are some huge issues that need to be resolved—and resolved quickly. The future of our home is at stake. America is on the verge of a make-it-or-break-it point. We have always had our ups and downs—that's just part of it—but right now we are experiencing some serious downs. I believe our situation is more serious than most of us know or even want to think about. However, we *must* think about it—and not only think about it, but also take action to correct it.

You may be like me, though. For a long time I have thought about it and have asked myself what I can do. How can I help turn this country around? I have no money. I have no power or influence. So what can I do? I'm just a common, everyday, blue-collar worker trying to survive. I watch the news, I read the newspaper, and all I see and hear about are problems and more problems: economics, jobs, politics, national security, and the list goes on and on.

Like most people, for a few years now, I have been worried, afraid, disgusted. At times, I've even thought it was all over—America is going down the drain. But again, I would think to myself, *What can I possibly do? There has to be something I can do, but I'm just one man out of three hundred million people.* That thought has burdened me beyond belief. The more I have talked with other people, the more I have realized the majority of Americans feel the same way. For the most part, I believe we are all afraid and worried. There is also a strong sense among everyday people of being helpless and hopeless. But let us not forget that we live in the land of hope! In spite of all of our troubles, this is still America.

One night it finally hit me. I was watching my son sleep. I sat next to his bed as I had many times before, but this time was different. Tears started filling my eyes and running down my face as I wondered what kind of America he would have to look forward to. What kind of future, if any, would he have in this country? So much has changed in the past ten years since September 11, 2001, and mostly not in good ways. I actually felt a sense of failing him. In my heart, I asked him to forgive me for not being able to promise him the America I had grown up knowing.

I left the room and went into the living room, where the flag that covered my dad's casket is displayed. I stared at that flag for what seemed like hours. I thought about my dad and the pride he had in serving his country and the love he had for this nation. As I stood there remembering him, I knew he had served this country for me. I knew he had served this country for my mom, my sister, and his grandkids. He served before my sister and I were ever born, but he knew even then his service was for the future of his children and the future of his family. Daddy did not let me down and I wish I could tell him that now.

In that moment, I knew I could not let my kids down, either. As an American and as their dad, it is my responsibility to do what I can, no matter how little or how much, to ensure that America is theirs for tomorrow. At this point, all I know to do is try to encourage and awaken others to the fact that this is still America, and together we can turn our country around. That is why I decided to write this book.

What you are about to read isn't coming from an Ivy League school graduate. My words may not be grand or philosophical. This isn't a novel filled with a wealth of knowledge, and it may not even be considered politically correct. It's simply a blue-collar, common man's point of view on a few subjects that affect all of us in some way. There are not going to be any ground-breaking ideas or congressional legislation, but simply a few commonsense ideas that I believe most Americans would agree with on how to help this great nation get back on its feet again and become the America we all need it to be.

I hope something you read on the following pages will inspire you in some way. I hope if you are feeling like I was, hopeless and powerless, that your heart will be stirred and your soul awakened to the fact that as Americans, we do have hope, we do have power. Our founding documents give each and every one of us those very things. Most important, they give us a voice, a voice which we can freely use. No matter how rich or how poor we are, or if we're somewhere in the middle, no matter what challenges we face, this is still America. It's the land of the free and home of the brave. It's the land where we, its people, have the authority to govern. It's the land where one can dream and freely pursue those dreams. I emphasize again, this is still America, so let us take it back while we can! The phrase "United we stand, divided we fall." has never been more relevant than it is today. So, let me pose the following questions: Where do you stand? What do you believe? Whatever your answers, may we all find some common ground and stand together as one. Let us stand as America and let the whole world see that we are stronger than ever, more united than ever, and that our colors never run. May the whole world see that America is here to stay!

Chapter 2

WHAT IS AMERICA?

Inaugural Address of President Ronald Reagan
Given on Tuesday, January 20, 1981

Senator Hatfield, Mr. Chief Justice, Mr. President, Vice President Bush, Vice President Mondale, Senator Baker, Speaker O'Neill, Reverend Moomaw, and my fellow citizens:

To a few of us here today, this is a solemn and most momentous occasion, and yet in the history of our nation, it is a commonplace occurrence. The orderly transfer of authority as called for in the Constitution routinely takes place, as it has for almost two centuries, and few of us stop to think how unique we really are. In the eyes of many in the world, this every-four-year ceremony we accept as normal is nothing less than a miracle.

Mr. President, I want our fellow citizens to know how much you did to carry on this tradition. By your gracious cooperation in the transition process, you have shown a watching world that we are a united people pledged to maintaining a political system which guarantees individual liberty to a greater degree than any other, and I thank you and your people for all your help in maintaining the continuity which is the bulwark of our Republic.

The business of our nation goes forward. These United States are confronted with an economic affliction of great proportions. We suffer from the longest and one of the worst sustained inflations in our national history. It distorts our economic decisions, penalizes thrift, and crushes the struggling young and the fixed-income elderly alike. It threatens to shatter the lives of millions of our people.

Idle industries have cast workers into unemployment, human misery, and personal indignity. Those who do work are denied a fair return for their labor by a tax system which penalizes successful achievement and keeps us from maintaining full productivity.

But great as our tax burden is, it has not kept pace with public spending. For decades, we have piled deficit upon deficit, mortgaging our future and our children's future for the temporary convenience of the present. To continue this long trend is to guarantee tremendous social, cultural, political, and economic upheavals.

You and I, as individuals, can, by borrowing, live beyond our means, but for only a limited period of time. Why, then, should we think that collectively, as a nation, we're not bound by that same limitation? We must act today in order to preserve tomorrow. And let there be no misunderstanding: We are going to begin to act, beginning today.

The economic ills we suffer have come upon us over several decades. They will not go away in days, weeks, or months, but they will go away. They will go away because we as Americans have the capacity now, as we've had in the past, to do whatever needs to be done to preserve this last and greatest bastion of freedom.

In this present crisis, government is not the solution to our problem; government is the problem. From time to time, we've been tempted to believe that society has become too complex to be managed by self-rule, that government by an elite group is superior to government for, by, and of the people. Well, if no one among us is capable of governing himself, then who among us has the capacity to govern someone else? All of us together, in and out of government, must bear the burden. The solutions we seek must be equitable, with no one group singled out to pay a higher price.

We hear much of special interest groups. Well, our concern must be for a special interest group that has been too long neglected. It knows no sectional boundaries or ethnic and racial divisions, and it crosses political party lines. It is made up of men and women who raise our food, patrol our streets, man our mines and factories, teach our children, keep our homes, and heal us when we're sick— professionals, industrialists, shopkeepers, clerks, cabbies, and truck drivers. They are, in short, "We the people," this breed called Americans.

Well, this administration's objective will be a healthy, vigorous, growing economy that provides equal opportunities for all Americans with no barriers born of bigotry or discrimination. Putting America back to work means putting all Americans back to work. Ending inflation means freeing all Americans from the terror of runaway living costs. All must share in the productive work of this "new beginning," and all must share in the bounty of a revived economy. With the idealism and fair play which are the core of our system and our strength, we can have a strong and prosperous America, at peace with itself and the world.

So, as we begin, let us take inventory. We are a nation that has a government—not the other way around. And this makes us special among the nations of the Earth. Our government has no power except that granted it by the people. It is time to check and reverse the growth of government, which shows signs of having grown beyond the consent of the governed.

It is my intention to curb the size and influence of the Federal establishment and to demand recognition of the distinction between the powers granted to the Federal Government and those reserved to the States or to the people. All of us need to be reminded that the Federal Government did not create the States; the States created the Federal Government.

Now, so there will be no misunderstanding, it's not my intention to do away with government. It is rather to make it work—work with us, not over us; to stand by our side, not ride on our back. Government can and must provide opportunity, not smother it; foster productivity, not stifle it.

If we look to the answer as to why for so many years we achieved so much, prospered as no other people on Earth, it was because here in this land we unleashed the energy and individual genius of man to a greater extent than has ever been done before. Freedom and the dignity of the individual have been more available and assured here than in any other place on Earth. The price for this freedom at times has been high, but we have never been unwilling to pay that price.

It is no coincidence that our present troubles parallel and are proportionate to the intervention and intrusion in our lives that result from unnecessary and excessive growth of government. It is time for us to realize that we're too great a nation to limit ourselves to small dreams. We're not, as some would have us believe, doomed to an inevitable decline. I do not believe in a fate that will fall on us no matter what we do. I do believe *in a fate that will fall on us if we do nothing. So, with all the creative energy at our command, let us begin an era of national renewal. Let us renew our determination, our courage, and our strength. And let us renew our faith and our hope.*

We have every right to dream heroic dreams. Those who say that we're in a time when there are not heroes, they just don't know where to look. You can see heroes every day, going in and out of factory gates. Others, a handful in number, produce enough food to feed all of us and then the world beyond. You meet heroes across a counter, and they're on both sides of that counter. There are entrepreneurs with faith in themselves and faith in an idea who create new jobs, new wealth and opportunity. They're individuals and families whose taxes support the government and whose voluntary gifts support church, charity, culture, art, and education. Their patriotism is quiet, but deep. Their values sustain our national life.

Now, I have used the words "they" and "their" in speaking of these heroes. I could say "you" and "your," because I'm addressing the heroes of whom I speak—you, the citizens of this blessed land. Your dreams, your hopes, your goals are going to be the dreams, the hopes, and the goals of this administration, so help me God.

We shall reflect the compassion that is so much a part of your makeup. How can we love our country and not love our countrymen; and loving them, reach out a hand when they fall, heal them when they're sick, and provide opportunity to make them self-sufficient so they will be equal in fact and not just in theory?

Can we solve the problems confronting us? Well, the answer is an unequivocal and emphatic "yes." To paraphrase Winston Churchill, I did not take the oath I've just taken with the intention of presiding over the dissolution of the world's strongest economy.

In the days ahead, I will propose removing the roadblocks that have slowed our economy and reduced productivity. Steps will be taken aimed at restoring the balance between the various levels of government. Progress may be slow, measured in inches and feet, not miles, but we will progress. It is time to reawaken this industrial giant, to get government back within its means, and to lighten our punitive tax burden. And these will be our first priorities, and on these principles there will be no compromise.

On the eve of our struggle for independence, a man who might have been one of the greatest among the Founding Fathers, Dr. Joseph Warren, president of the Massachusetts Congress, said to his fellow Americans, "Our country is in danger, but not to be despaired of ... On you depend the fortunes of America. You are to decide the important questions upon which rests the happiness and the liberty of millions yet unborn. Act worthy of yourselves."

Well, I believe we, the Americans of today, are ready to act worthy of ourselves, ready to do what must be done to ensure happiness and liberty for ourselves, our children, and our children's children. And as we renew ourselves here in our own land, we will be seen as having greater strength throughout the world. We will again be the exemplar of freedom and a beacon of hope for those who do not now have freedom.

To those neighbors and allies who share our freedom, we will strengthen our historic ties and assure them of our

*support and firm commitment. We will match loyalty
with loyalty. We will strive for mutually beneficial
relations. We will not use our friendship to impose on their
sovereignty, for our own sovereignty is not for sale.*

*As for the enemies of freedom, those who are potential
adversaries, they will be reminded that peace is the highest
aspiration of the American people. We will negotiate for it,
sacrifice for it; we will not surrender for it, now or ever.*

*Our forbearance should never be misunderstood. Our
reluctance for conflict should not be misjudged as a failure
of will. When action is required to preserve our national
security, we will act. We will maintain sufficient strength
to prevail if need be, knowing that if we do so, we have
the best chance of never having to use that strength.*

*Above all, we must realize that no arsenal or no weapon in
the arsenals of the world is so formidable as the will and
moral courage of free men and women. It is a weapon our
adversaries in today's world do not have. It is a weapon that
we as Americans do have. Let that be understood by those
who practice terrorism and prey upon their neighbors.*

*I'm told that tens of thousands of prayer meetings are being
held on this day, and for that I'm deeply grateful. We are a
nation under God, and I believe God intended for us to be
free. It would be fitting and good, I think, if on each Inaugural
Day in future years, it should be declared a day of prayer.*

*This is the first time in our history that this ceremony has been
held, as you've been told, on this West Front of the Capitol.*

Standing here, one faces a magnificent vista, opening up on this city's special beauty and history. At the end of this open mall are those shrines to the giants on whose shoulders we stand.

Directly in front of me, the monument to a monumental man, George Washington, father of our country. A man of humility who came to greatness reluctantly. He led America out of revolutionary victory into infant nationhood. Off to one side, the stately memorial to Thomas Jefferson. The Declaration of Independence flames with his eloquence. And then, beyond the Reflecting Pool, the dignified columns of the Lincoln Memorial. Whoever would understand in his heart the meaning of America will find it in the life of Abraham Lincoln.

Beyond those monuments to heroism is the Potomac River, and on the far shore, the sloping hills of Arlington National Cemetery, with its row upon row of simple white markers bearing crosses or Stars of David. They add up to only a tiny fraction of the price that has been paid for our freedom.

Each one of those markers is a monument to the kind of hero I spoke of earlier. Their lives ended in places called Belleau Wood, The Argonne, Omaha Beach, Salerno, and halfway around the world on Guadalcanal, Tarawa, Pork Chop Hill, the Chosin Reservoir, and in a hundred rice paddies and jungles of a place called Vietnam.

Under one such marker lies a young man, Martin Treptow, who left his job in a small town barbershop in 1917 to go to France with the famed Rainbow Division. There, on the western front, he was killed trying to carry a message between battalions under heavy artillery fire.

We're told that on his body was found a diary. On the flyleaf under the heading, "My Pledge," he had written these words: "America must win this war. Therefore I will work, I will save, I will sacrifice, I will endure, I will fight cheerfully and do my utmost, as if the issue of the whole struggle depended on me alone."

The crisis we are facing today does not require of us the kind of sacrifice that Martin Treptow and so many thousands of others were called upon to make. It does require, however, our best effort and our willingness to believe in ourselves and to believe in our capacity to perform great deeds, to believe that together with God's help, we can and will resolve the problems which now confront us.

And after all, why shouldn't we believe that? We are Americans.

God bless you, and thank you.

I have thought about this question a lot as I have gotten older and seen the changes taking place in our country. As I think about what America is to me, I think back to when I was a child. I can remember going to baseball games and, as our national anthem played, every hand and hat was over every heart in the stadium as every person stood and faced our flag. There was no laughing, no talking, no texting or cell phones ringing. There was nothing but a few moments of quiet reverence as we honored the flag that represents us to the rest of the world, and all it symbolizes.

I also remember, as every four years rolled around, the Olympics. I remember when the Olympic Games seemed to be as big as the Super Bowl is today. Families and friends would gather around the television to watch as our athletes competed to bring home the ultimate prize, the cherished gold medal. However, that wasn't the only prize. For me and millions of others, the ultimate prize was watching our flag being raised in that top, middle position as our national anthem was played for the whole world to witness. What pride that brought to everyone! Both young and old alike shared goose bumps and tears as the red, white, and blue was lifted high.

I remember too in school, every morning began with the Pledge of Allegiance and a prayer. How simple it was, but every day, in just a few minutes, we honored and remembered two basic principles this country was founded on: God and freedom. Isn't it sad how things have changed? In some places it is now illegal to even mention the name of God, and yet we wonder why we are heading down this road we're on. That's another topic, though, that I will cover in the next chapter.

America, have you ever really taken the time to stop and think about this land we call home? Have you ever thought about what America is? Most of us probably haven't. Most of us just go about our daily routines, caught up in the hustle and bustle of our fast-paced modern society, and never give it a second thought. Sure, we see the American flag displayed in various places: high up on a flagpole, draped from the side of a building, in weathered paint on the side of a barn. Occasionally you'll see Old Glory flapping in the wind as it's carried in the back of a truck that's barreling down the highway, but what does it really mean? What constitutes this displaying of our national flag? Pride? Maybe. Speaking of the displaying and flying of flags, what ever happened to the days and months after 9/11? Stores couldn't keep flags on their shelves because they were selling out so fast. Now, you see flags on shelves that are on clearance because the *patriotic holidays* are over and it's time to move on to a new season. I didn't think there was such a thing as patriotic seasons. I've always thought patriotism was year-round. It is something that should always be alive and well, no matter what season it is, no matter what else is going on. So, I suppose that brings me back to the question, what is America?

Well, America is many things to many people, and it would be foolish of me to assume I could answer that question for anyone else but me, so that is what I'm going to do. I'm going to offer you what America means to me, a common man, and maybe, just maybe, no matter who you are, we will find some common ground together in this uncommon country.

These are just a few things I think about when I ask myself, "What is America?" and I'm sure you can think of several things yourself, but then I wonder what gave us the ability to have them in the first place?

I look around at our cities and marvel at all of the engineering and hard work it takes to construct them. I think about the years it has taken for them to be built and all that goes into growing those cities. I see roads and major highways traveling here and there, and as I look at them wherever they may exist, I think to myself, *That is America, a land of big cities and bright lights.* I see our big cities as signs of our prosperity. I, like many others, view them as havens of humanity. I realize though I am wrong in thinking that way because our big cities aren't who we are. Though they represent our prosperity and strength, they are not America. America is the people who have built those cities and roads. America is also the spirit that lives inside those people. Before the first shovel ever dug or bulldozer cleared land, before a pencil was ever put to paper to design or money loaned to build, there was a dream. There was a dream and a determination to make sure America was and would be a land where people could work hard and succeed. There was a dream and determination to ensure all people, no matter what their background or position in life, could achieve whatever their hearts desired. There was a dream and determination that America would be the best and set the standard for humanity the world over. And now, America is the people who inhabit our cities. America is the people who live and work in those places to keep the dream of prosperity alive. The easy part is already done. The buildings are there. The conveniences are there. It is up to us, the people who live in our cities, to ensure the dream and determination to build them never dies. From the mailroom to the boardroom, let us listen to each other and work with each other to make America what it should always be, a land of true opportunity and reward.

After thinking about our cities, my thoughts move on to the country and our farmland. As far as the eye can see, there are crops: corn, wheat, beans, tomatoes, and the list goes on and on. I think of how blessed our land has always been to be capable of providing food for us. So many places can't claim that about their land. I see barns and silos, all of the heavy tractors and other equipment it takes to run those farms, and it seems to me that that is America as well. Once again, though, I recognize that what I'm seeing on the surface isn't America. All of the crops are wonderful. They are a blessing to us, but America is the farmers raising those crops and the ranchers raising cattle and other livestock on their land. America is that drive, that spirit that wakes them up every single morning and motivates them to work their land and raise their livestock. America is that sense of responsibility they have to feed the rest of us. When was the last time you thought about where your last meal came from or where your next one would be coming from? Well, thank your fellow Americans, the farmer and the rancher. We have a long and proud history in both of those areas, and we need to celebrate it. From sun up to sun down, they work hard to make sure we have food. Just as those who have built and continue to build our cities, these farmers and ranchers work tireless, thankless, and selfless hours to ensure our survival and prosperity. All of these people are America, and on behalf of my fellow citizens I thank you.

As I continue to think about what America is, I think about all of the monuments that have been built and statues erected. This country is covered with them. From the East Coast to the West, and the northern border to the southern, there are monuments of all kinds. There are those few popular ones that tour buses stop at and people visit during their travels, but most of the time our monuments are just passed by and ignored. A really popular thing I've noticed is the naming of bridges and roads in memory or honor of someone or some historical event. But what are they all really for? What do they really mean? They are obviously not America, but I believe if we slowed down a little and took some time to read the plaques that have been placed, we would learn that who and what they symbolize is America. If we just took the time, we would see that these statues, monuments, and anything else placed in honor or memory actually tells the story of America. All of these things are here to help remind us of where we come from. They have been placed to let us know that we are here today because of the hopes, courage, and sacrifices of those who dared to pursue the dream of America.

I believe we can all relate to at least one of these examples. In thinking and writing about them, it made me stop looking so much at the *what* and opened my eyes more to the *who* behind it all. Maybe you can do the same. The way I see it, America is not the things that we have; it is not our luxuries and wealth. We, the people, are America! We are a tapestry of ideas and beliefs, of history and heritage, saturated with hopes and dreams. Each piece is stitched together by a common thread: the bond of the pursuit of happiness and freedom.

For over two hundred years now, the people who have occupied this land have been America, and the road they have traveled has certainly not been an easy or perfect one. Many tears and much blood have been shed. Countless lives have been lost on our soil and abroad. Many moral and civil boundaries have been crossed and broken down. Even today, we still struggle with some of the same prejudices and biases we have always had. People say that's just human nature, and even though that may be true, there is nothing that opened minds can't conquer. I believe, as Americans, we are called to overcome the excuse of human nature. To be the America we need to be, we have no choice but to accept that responsibility and look past our differences to find what we have in common so we can make this nation work. So many other nations have not and will not do that, and that is why they fail. We can respect one another's differences and still pursue our common goals. We can be tolerant without sacrificing our founding principles and beliefs. The hard part is doing it, but we must! That is one thing that has made this nation great and one reason so many people have sought to come here. I believe it is a great testament to all we have here that countless people from around the world have risked everything, including their lives and the lives of their loved ones, to come here.

Even though we have our problems right now, America is still the greatest nation to have ever existed in the history of mankind. However, we are currently facing a crucial and defining moment in time. With the ever-increasing number of policies leading us away from our liberty and principles, it is essential that we remember who we are, where we come from, and where we want to go. We must first and foremost remember we were founded on freedom. Freedom for the individual gave birth to the freedom of a nation, and in no way, form, or fashion should we give any of that freedom up to anyone or anything—and that includes our own government!

Another thing to remember is that in spite of our current situation, we are still a land of hopes and dreams. It is a lot harder right now than in times past, but we have always triumphed over whatever may have been in our way. Because of our ability to hope and dream we, as individuals and as a nation, are able to declare that. You may know someone who has given up on hope, and if you do, make it your aspiration to lift them up and give them hope! Who knows, you may even lift yourself up in the process. As the saying goes, "Be the change you want to see in others and around you." We have to help one another. Had we not done so in the past, we would not be here today. Part of being an American is having the capacity to see past yourself and look out for those around you. That is a concept that almost seems to be forgotten about today: helping others. Generations before us *had* to help each other and sacrifice. I believe we are at a point today where we need to be the next generation of help and sacrifice to ensure the survival of this nation.

That brings up another topic. America is a generous nation. As a nation, we help more people around the world than anyone else. When disaster strikes, who gets the call? America. Why? Because that is also a part of who we are and what we stand for. We have always tried to help those who can't help themselves. Sometimes we have been misguided and placed resources in the wrong hands, but we have always been a nation that gives. As far as money and food, we give and have given more than anyone else in history. But we have also given more in the cost of lives to help spread freedom and humanity around the world. Even though we have always tried to help others, I believe now more than ever we need to help ourselves first. How can we advance those causes to others if we are slowly losing them here at home? We need to feed our people and secure our freedom first because if we want America to have a prosperous future, we must first prosper here and now. We have babies, veterans, and every sort and age of person in between starving on our own streets. That is an inexcusable disgrace. Now more than ever, we need each other in order to survive. Now more than ever, we need America.

So, let me ask again, what is America? America is you and me. America is that uncompromising spirit that will not tolerate evil but fights for what is right and for those who cannot fight for themselves. Evil comes in all forms, but no matter what form it comes in, America will prevail over it. America is also that determined spirit that says when you get knocked down, get back up again. It is that unrelenting drive that says good isn't always good enough. America is the power that we all have in our hands, given to us by our Creator and our Founding Fathers, to make life what we choose to make it. America is a continuous work in progress, constantly pursuing perfection. It is still a land where one can dream and make that dream a reality. America is all of this and so much more. Ultimately, it all comes back to you and me. We, the people, are America. What will we make it? Hopefully, we will make it and leave it a better place than it was when we got here.

I'm a person who believes music can be a powerful force. Songs can say a lot in a short time. I'm going to give you some of the lyrics to a handful of songs throughout this book that I believe help define who and what we are as a nation. Some of the songs you may have heard and others maybe not. Either way, if you need a patriotic boost, I encourage you to not only let their lyrics stir you, but seek out the songs and really listen to them. I believe the songs I have chosen to share here will help sum up what I have tried to convey. The first song is from the country music group Alabama, entitled "Forty Hour Week." I believe this song captures the overall spirit of the blue-collar worker in America and truly represents the core of American life.

"For the waitress, the mechanic, the policeman on patrol
For everyone who works behind the scenes
With a spirit you can't replace with no machine
Hello America let me thank you for your time"

Chapter 3

GOD AND COUNTRY

Blessed is the nation whose God is the LORD;
and the people whom he hath chosen
for his own inheritance.

-Psalm 33:12 KJV

If my people, which are called by my name,
shall humble themselves, and pray, and seek my face,
and turn from their wicked ways;
then will I hear from heaven, and will forgive
their sin, and will heal their land.

-II Chronicles 7:14 KJV

The more you listen, the more you hear young and old, rich and poor ask what we need to do in order to turn this country around. The first thing we need to do as a country to turn ourselves and our future around is to turn back to God. That is where we need to start. I believe that with my whole heart.

I believe that because faith is where we began in the first place. Sometimes, when circumstances may seem too overwhelming or out of control, we need to simply go back to the basics—in our case, God. No matter how you want to look at it, our founders had a very strong, unshakable faith in God. They had to in order to take the leap of faith to leave England and risk life itself in pursuit of a land they could call home—a land in which they would break the chains of tyranny so they could worship almighty God openly and freely. There is no disputing that. And it was through their faith they were able to come here and establish the cornerstone that would build the nation we have become.

Granted, it has not always been perfect. Nothing is or ever will be when human beings are involved. There have been and always will be people who, when given the authority of any kind, will abuse the privilege. That is just how it is. There are people who will always take things to the extreme in order to achieve their own personal agendas. However, in the case of God, sooner or later those who abuse what He has given them will be removed, and the wrong that has been done will be made right. It may not happen in the time or in the way we want, but it will happen. Ultimately, God is the judge of all things and all people. We must remember that.

Evil will always try to pervert good in order to distract from the truth. However, when night seems the darkest and coldest, the dawning of a new day is at hand. The darkness fades as the sun rises. This is the place we absolutely must return to in this country. We must remember that through God, we are the light. Not by our own power or will, but by the power He has given us to do His will. God gave the world this gift called America, and we have to preserve it. He gave us the honor and privilege of being born here or the ability to immigrate here. He also gave us free will. Through the blood shed by His son, Jesus, and that of all who have died in service to this country, we have freedom, and we need to use the free will He gave us to protect it. You can live anywhere and have freedom in Christ, but America also allows you to worship God freely and openly without fear of death or persecution. We have what I call double freedom. However, that is in great jeopardy. That is why we need to get back to the basics and remember where we come from.

Something I find very disturbing is all the rhetoric about fundamentally changing America. If you really listen to a lot of the socialist groups and some politicians, you will hear that kind of talk. The reason this is so disturbing is because when they speak of fundamental changes, they are speaking of trying to change the very principles this country was founded on. The most notable change to our principles is our nation's founding belief in God. Just look at the last ten years and all of the lawsuits and proposed legislation on both state and federal levels to ban prayers, Bibles, and the use of the name of God. All of this is an all-out attack on the core of America. The sad part is that it seems to mostly go unnoticed. Even sadder is that the courts in place to uphold our principles are slowly, piece by piece, giving up this great nation. We should be outraged!

Whether you believe in God or not, I challenge you to research our history. Look at the time just before the 1960s and then compare that to our times now. You will see that before prayer started being banned, America was mostly a whole nation. We didn't have divorce and suicide rates running wild. We didn't have problems with drugs and alcohol abuse like we do now. Families were together. Our education system was intact and the best in the world. America was prosperous. Look at us now. Fifty years later, we are the laughing stock of the world. Fifty years before the 1960s, we were the envy of the world. Why? Because we were a nation that put God first, and we weren't afraid to. President Lincoln said, "The philosophy of the schoolroom of one generation will be the philosophy of government in the next." Look at us, again from the 1960s till now. Can you imagine the next generation of government? We need to turn back to God now while we still can.

Some may say they don't believe in God or their religion believes in someone or something other than the God of the Bible. That's fine. That's one of the great parts of America; we can worship how we want, if we want. We can freely choose who and what to believe in. Our Constitution provides for that. However, there are house rules or, at least, there should be. I know this is a touchy subject for some, and those people will likely disagree with me, but that's okay.

Our Forefathers had an abiding belief in the one true God of the Bible and created the foundation of this country in His likeness. Our God has given us freewill to make our own choices in life. Even though He wants us to follow Him, we have to choose for ourselves if we will accept Him or reject Him. He does nothing to stand in the way of our choices. Similarly, even though our Founding Fathers knew there is only one true God, they incorporated into our founding documents freedom of religion, allowing us the ability to choose if and who we will worship. They could have made it mandatory for us to follow in their religious footsteps, but because of their belief in God, they followed His model and allowed for us to have the right to worship how we want to, if at all. Our freedom of religion, no matter what religion that is, stems from the strong belief and faith our Forefathers had in God. To state that more simply, in America you may choose your own religion or reject it altogether, but please have the decency to acknowledge and respect the fact that it was and is our basis in Christian beliefs that makes that possible for you.

Some say Christianity is hateful and non-tolerant. Some say Christianity is outdated and close-minded. However, Christianity won't cut your head off if you choose not to conform. Christianity won't imprison you if you choose to read something other than the Bible. Christianity won't burn your house down and murder your family because you won't believe and swear allegiance to Christ. As a matter of fact, if you read the Bible, you will see that God is a God of love. He is a God of second chances. Christianity is a religion of peace because God is peace. No God, no peace. Know God, know peace. Sure, there are rights and wrongs. What faith doesn't have those? There are things He requires of us, but only for our own good. Love one another; do unto others as you would have done unto you; forgive your bother—just to name a few. He doesn't tell us to lie and deceive in order to convert others. He doesn't tell us to kill those who will not follow.

I know one of the big topics today is homosexuality. Believe it or not, true Christianity doesn't call for the death of homosexuals. However, Islam does. Ultimately, God is the judge of us all. He gives His guidelines in the Bible and leaves it up to us to follow them or not. Of course, if you don't choose Him, the alternative will be unbearable, but He leaves it up to us, the individual. We decide our fate, not our fellow man. It's really incredible when you think that Christianity is considered a religion of hate. I know we all see things differently, and that's okay. That is another great part of being an American. We can have different points of view on religion and not have to live in fear. So in light of that, let us look at the following.

Christianity is considered, I'll say it again, intolerant and close-minded, but let's look at another religion. How about Islam? I know there are many peaceful Muslims. Let me be clear about that. However, when you compare those of different religions around the world— Christian, Catholic, Jew, Muslim, for example—who is doing what to whom in the name of their religion? We don't hear about it in our mainstream media, but Christians are murdered all over the world in the name of Islam. Muslims are killing other Muslims because they are of a different tribe. Something you do see in the media is that Iran and other Muslim states want to totally annihilate Israel in the name of Islam. Also, right here in America, we see more and more beatings and killings of Muslim kids and women because they are becoming westernized.

They are called honor killings. Well, first of all, they moved here; we didn't move to where they lived. If they don't want to become westernized, they don't need to move here. It's just that simple. I ask this though: what kind of religion is considered peaceful and loving but then finds honor in a believer murdering family members because they stepped a little out of bounds of the perimeters of their religion? If that is peaceful and loving, I'll do without.

My point is that it's not hard to see, if you let yourself, which religions of the world are really about love and peace and which aren't. Here is another thought: if your religion can't co-exist with Christianity or the Constitution, then you don't need to be here. That may sound cold and contradictory to other things I've said, but as a nation, we can only be tolerant to a certain point. We have made a mistake by being too tolerant and allowing other beliefs to come in and start tearing down the walls of our house so they can build up what they want. In order to preserve America, we have to safeguard our history, our principles, our Constitution, and our basic founding beliefs. And sometimes in order to preserve what we have, we have to say no. We have to draw the line somewhere.

Suppose you were to let someone come live in your home. You'd probably have certain guidelines you'd make them live by. If they didn't, you'd kick them out. So, why do you have guidelines at your house? To preserve your household and the way you do things. Also, you don't want someone coming in and destroying or stealing everything you've worked so hard for. It's the same way with our country. America is our home. There has been a lot of work and sacrifice by millions to make it our home. We must preserve it. Unfortunately, we are allowing others to come in and twist and turn our rules against us, and we should have the guts to say no. If those we elect aren't preserving and fighting for our way of life, then it is up to us, the people, to do so. Not with violence, but with the rights and power given to us by our Constitution and our God. We must remove those in power and replace them with individuals who have the fortitude and foresight of our Forefathers to ensure America truly stays the land of the free.

Something is dreadfully wrong when prayer and Bibles are banned, but prayer rugs are allowed. Something is dreadfully wrong when "One nation under God" is taken out of our Pledge of Allegiance and we stand in silence. Something is dreadfully wrong in a land where we are supposed to be a Christian nation and the only time we get on our knees is to apologize for who and what we are instead of being on our knees praying to God Almighty to help us become who and what we need to be. America, something is dreadfully wrong, and we need—no, we must—change it now! Wake up, America! If we don't wake up now, when we do, America will just be a dream. We have to get back to the basics.

Whether or not you are a Christian and believe in the Bible, I challenge you to study it. Look in the Bible and see what happened when those who once believed in God, whether an individual or a nation, turned away from Him. When we turn from God, we *will* fall. Sometimes we'll get back up; sometimes we won't. That is up to us. He is always there for us. Again, He is not going to make us want Him. He wants us to want Him. The bottom line is this: since the early 1960s America has been turning her back on God. Eventually, no matter how great we are, if we don't turn back, we will fall.

So, what are we going to do? It all starts with us. Are we going to continue down this road or are we going to turn our face toward God and ask for forgiveness for what we haven't done and the strength to do what needs to be done? I say again, let us as a nation turn back to God. Let us get back to our roots before our roots are forever cut away. Now is the time, America, now is the time. Being Christian doesn't mean we are weak. Being Christian doesn't mean we always have to give in. Being Christian and being American means we can fight when we need to. We can and should make a stand. Being Christian and being American means we help those who can't help themselves. Being Christian and being American means we look past the here and now to tomorrow and beyond, and do what is right no matter the costs.

> *What shall we then say to these things?*
> *If GOD be for us, who can be against us?*
>
> -Romans 8:31 KJV

> *GOD is our refuge and strength,*
> *a very present help in trouble.*
>
> - Psalm 46:1 KJV

I know many of you reading this don't believe in God. I also know if you don't, you have your reasons. I know people have many questions about God and Christianity, inside and outside of the Christian faith. One of the most common questions is why does God allow bad things to happen to good people? There are so many more questions, but I'm not going to attempt to answer any of them because I don't have all of the answers myself. Besides, we all have our own views anyway. All I am trying to say is let us get back to the simple basics that we can unite on and move forward.

Even if you aren't of the Christian faith, I believe there are things that bind us together simply by being fellow Americans. Those things stem from the roots of Christianity—actually the very teachings of Jesus himself. There are those simple things, such as love and compassion. Then there are other things, such as standing up against evil and corruption, fighting for and taking care of those who can't defend or take care of themselves. Examples include feeding the hungry, clothing those who have nothing, and helping to house the homeless. These simple things are some of the greatest characteristics that define who we are as a nation.

Christian, Jew, Catholic, Atheist, or whatever you are, my whole point is that we need to focus on the basic values that we have in common to start restoring this great nation. We will always disagree on religion and politics to some degree, but no matter your faith, there is no disputing that our founding principles worked then, and they will work today. Even if you don't believe in God, for whatever reason—and I do really hope you would come to believe in Him—but if for nothing else than your belief in America, let us all work together with what we have in common, and the rest will work itself out.

I personally have learned that some of my greatest disappointments have come when I put too much faith in myself and man, and not enough in God. I'm not saying not to have faith in our fellow man and ourselves, because we need to—just not too much. If we base our whole outlook on Christianity in man, we will never see all of God's goodness because man can and will fail. God will not.

America is unique and most blessed out of all of the nations on earth for having the religious freedom we do. In order for us to stay blessed, we have to preserve it the way it was founded. Some say our founding beliefs are outdated. Well, I do know this: anytime a major building is erected there is always a cornerstone, a foundation. Once that building is complete, if you remove that cornerstone, the building will fall. That cornerstone is put in place to help ensure the building stays strong and lasts a long time. Even though it ages and may get a little weathered, as long as that cornerstone stays in place, so will the building. The same goes for our founding principles. It just so happens that God is our cornerstone. If we remove Him, we will fall. If we keep Him where He needs to be, we will continue to stand strong.

I know earlier I stated that if your beliefs can't co-exist with America's founding beliefs, you might need to go elsewhere. Well, that's not meant to degrade anyone's beliefs, but if it is true that your faith can't honestly co-exist with America, then you aren't being true to yourself or your beliefs anyway by being here. If you want our way of life, you need to conform to America. "That goes against freedom of religion," you may say. Does it really? No one is saying you can't worship how you want; you do have that freedom. But again, are you really being true to yourself and your faith? Only you can answer that.

Even with all of our freedom, we must still draw certain lines to protect that freedom and liberty. It amazes me how America is always condemned for being intolerant, especially when we bend over backward to accommodate any and all religions and languages that are present here. How many other countries around the world will publish schoolbooks, periodicals, and countless other pieces of literature in dozens and dozens of languages because people can't speak their native language? In our case, that's English. How many other countries can people go to with a hope of having better lives and pursue their dreams? How many other countries can you go to and openly and freely practice whatever religion you may have chosen, without being afraid? Not many. So, with those few things in mind, again I say, let us remember, honor, cherish, and practice our founding principles to ensure a future America with bigger dreams and more prosperity than ever.

I close this chapter by leaving you with a few words of a song entitled "America Again," written by a Christian artist named Carman. He wrote and released this in the 1990s, but it is just as relevant today as it was then, maybe even more so. I encourage you to find the song and listen to it. I believe you will get a real blessing and revived spirit after hearing it. May God bless you, and may God bless America.

"I believe it's time for America to stand up and proclaim
That one nation under God is our demand
And send this evil lifestyle back to Satan
where it came from
And let the Word of God revive our dying land"

Chapter 4
RESPECT

R-E-S-P-E-C-T! This is a word that really seems to have lost its meaning. Nowadays, the only time people seem to want to use this word is when it pertains to them. So many people are concerned about being disrespected. Everyone wants respect, but it's something that has to be earned. Sure, we need to respect each other as fellow citizens and human beings, but things have gotten to the point where others think you have disrespected them if you have looked at them the wrong way, or if you disagree with them, you have disrespected them. Get a grip! If everyone gave as much respect as they demanded, things would probably be a lot different. People want it, but don't always want to give it.

That brings me back to a point I made previously: being an American is a privilege, not a right. Far too often, we forget that. We take for granted that many have died and continue to in order for us to have that privilege. So, as far as respect goes, first and foremost, I believe we need to respect America for being the unique and privileged place it is. After all, it is our home. We all need to respect those who have served this nation. If anyone has earned and deserves respect, it is them. It is because of their service and sacrifice that we are able to call America our home in the first place.

The thing we cherish the most as Americans, our freedom, has come with a heavy price. Thousands of people have laid down their lives to give us what we have today. Millions have served and sacrificed because of the love and appreciation they have for our country. Not only have our soldiers sacrificed, but their families have as well, and we often forget that. According to the Department of Defense's 2010 Demographics Report profiling the military community, there are close to 2 million family members of the active duty military personnel. That is made up of more than 725,000 spouses and approximately 1.25 million children, while other non-children dependents constitute the remainder.[1] Husbands, wives, children, family—when one serves, they all serve. In that service, many families have been forever changed because of the loss of a loved one in combat or training, while many more have received devastating injuries. Either way, whatever the loss, it happened during service to this nation in the never-ending battle to preserve America. It happened during their service for you and me.

Not only are extreme sacrifices made, but daily sacrifices as well, things that non-military families take for granted every day. Ballgames, recitals, birthday parties, the very birth of a child are just a few examples, as is sitting down to dinner or just going to the store together. When a member is gone in service to our country, the whole family gives. Children don't understand why Mommy has to go away, and it's not easy for anyone left behind to explain it to them. When Daddy comes home after being gone for a long time and he's not quite the same because of all he's seen and experienced, the entire family has to work things through to get life back to normal or as close to normal as possible. Things such as reading a bedtime story or going fishing are missed. Countless milestones that will never happen again are missed. There are

---

[1]   "Demographics 2010 Profile of the Military Community," MilitaryHOMEFRONT, accessed March 4, 2012, http://www.militaryhomefront.dod.mil//12038/Project%20Documents/MilitaryHOMEFRONT/Reports/2010_Demographics_Report.pdf.

so many more examples, and I've just barely scratched the surface. The sacrifices are many, and for what? Ultimately, the sacrifices made by all of our soldiers and their families are for the defense and preservation of our way of life, our freedom, our America.

Think about the following. Currently our population is around 313 million. According to the Department of Defense's Military Homefront website and their 2010 Demographics Report, we have around 1.4 million active duty members and approximately 1 million more in reserves.[2] They are those who protect and keep the freedom for the other 310 million of us. So, again, if anyone deserves respect, it is them: the men, women, and families of our armed forces. If they didn't serve, we wouldn't be here. At the very least, I believe the rest of us should live in a manner that ensures their sacrifices are not in vain. We should live in a way that shows we not only honor and respect them, but we honor and respect the freedom they preserve. One way we can honor and respect their sacrifices is to continue the prosperous growth of this great nation. If we do that, then when they need us, we will have the resources to serve them as they have served us. I believe that is just the right thing to do. So, on behalf of all freedom-loving Americans, if you are a soldier or a family member of a soldier, thank you and may God bless you.

---

2   "Demographics 2010 Profile of the Military Community," MilitaryHOMEFRONT, accessed March 4, 2012, http://www. militaryhomefront.dod.mil//12038/Project%20Documents/ MilitaryHOMEFRONT/Reports/2010_Demographics_Report. pdf.

If you haven't heard the song "American Soldier" by country music superstar, Toby Keith, I encourage you to listen to it. I believe it perfectly describes our soldiers and their sacrifices. Here are just a few of the meaningful lyrics.

"And I will always do my duty
no matter what the price
I've counted up the cost, I know the sacrifice
Oh and I don't want to die for you,
but if dyin's asked of me
I'll bear that cross with honor,
cause freedom don't come free."

So, how do we respect our nation and the sacrifices made by all who have served? The first thing we do is learn how not to take America for granted. It is so easy today for us to overlook what we have here. We have so many conveniences and comforts that we often seem to forget that others around the world aren't so fortunate. Sure, we need to celebrate and enjoy what we do have, but at the same time, we should be humble about it. Respect lies in being humble and gracious for what we have. For in the humility of knowing the true treasure we have in America, we will find the honor in doing what is necessary to ensure that future generations will be able to have what we have today and even more. I use the word *humility* because without it, arrogance will plant its roots and, like poison ivy, will spread as far as it can, choking and killing whatever it may attach itself to.

It's not hard to look back and see how arrogance has caused kings to lose their thrones and nations to fall. Being humble doesn't mean we're weak. Being humble about the many blessings we have in America means we recognize our greatness and what it has taken to get us here. In light of that, we know what it takes to keep this treasure called America and secure it for the future.

I believe the second thing is to simply respect each other. If we can't respect each other as fellow citizens in our own land, there's no way the world will respect us as a nation. I can't imagine how much better off we all would be if we would just respect each other as fellow human beings. Why is it so hard for us to focus on what we all have in common and work together to accomplish what needs to be done, instead of just focusing on our differences? Pride and arrogance, that's why. We are so busy trying to be right in the eyes of others and in our own minds that we become paralyzed into not doing what is right. Do unto others as you would have done unto you: there's a reason that saying is known as the Golden Rule. It seems we have gotten to a point in America where we will go out of the way to do what we know to be wrong instead of just doing some simple, random act of kindness.

What about something as basic as holding the door open for someone else? What about letting someone over into your lane of traffic instead of going all out to cut them off? What about just a simple thank you? Here's one for you: have you ever been in line at the grocery store and all you have is five small items but the person in front of you has about fifty? Have you stood there thinking, *Couldn't you let me go first instead of making me wait fifteen minutes to check out?* If you're honest about it, I bet you have. We all have. Remember that the next time you have a full cart and the person behind you is holding a gallon of milk and a loaf of bread. Kindness can be contagious: if we participate in random acts of kindness, chances are the recipients of our actions will pay it forward to others, leading to a domino effect. The bottom line is we all have a desire to feel respected and by showing kindness to others you are ultimately showing them respect. Keep in mind what goes around, comes around. If you want respect, give respect, but do it graciously.

"There is no experience better for the heart than reaching down and lifting people up."

-John Andrew Holmer

"The smallest act of kindness is worth more than the grandest intention."

-Anonymous

"There are no unimportant jobs, no unimportant people, no unimportant acts of kindness."

-Anonymous

After all, we are all trying to do pretty much the same thing anyway. We are all trying to make a living the best way we can in order to have a roof over our heads and food in our stomachs. We are all trying to live and survive. I believe one of the best ways I've ever heard it said was by President Kennedy in his speech given at the American University in Washington DC on June 10, 1963:

"For in the final analysis, our most basic common link, is that we all inhabit this small planet, we all breathe the same air,

we all cherish our children's futures,
and we are all mortal."

-President John F. Kennedy

I also believe that one of our best moments in time for respecting and caring for one another was during one of our worst moments in time, September 11, 2001. For the first few months following, even though we may not have known each other's names, I don't believe there were any strangers at all in this country. We were one nation, one people. The color of your skin didn't matter, nor did the amount of money in your pocketbook. We stood together as one, all working and pushing in the same direction: forward. Unfortunately, it took that kind of tragedy to pull us together. More unfortunate, though, is that the unity and respect didn't last, and I just don't understand it. We actually seem more selfish and disrespectful today than we did before those attacks took place. How quickly we forget, as individuals and as a nation that nothing is guaranteed, but death. Our health isn't guaranteed. Our money isn't guaranteed. Our very freedom and nation isn't guaranteed unless we can get back to the basics of how we treat each other and our country.

If you have never heard the song by country music superstar Alan Jackson, "Where Were You (When the World Stopped Turning)," I strongly encourage you to listen to it. I believe it sums up how America felt on September 11, but even more important, I believe it gives us a reminder of some basic fundamentals of who we are as a people. I leave you with a few of his words.

"Did you burst out in pride for the red, white & blue
And the heroes who died just doin' what they do?
Did you look up to heaven for some kind of answer
And look at yourself and what really matters?"

In summary, we have no choice but to respect each other to ensure the survival of America. Again, it all starts with the individual. We must first respect ourselves for who we are. Don't ever sell yourself short. No matter how bad of a place you may be in, there is always a way out. We have opportunity in this nation if we try. I'm not saying it will be an easy road, but there is still opportunity and hope if we choose to see it. Once we can respect ourselves, then, and only then, will we be able to respect others and this great nation of ours. We, as individuals, have to rise above our own circumstances so we, as a nation, can do the same. It is our obligation as Americans to offer a hand of help if we see others struggling and, if we can help, try to better the lives of our fellow human beings. That in turn will only make this nation stronger. We all want respect, so how much of it are we willing to give?

Webster's Dictionary defines respect as:
1. to feel or show honor for; think highly of; look up
to 2. to be thoughtful about; have regard for

"I expect to pass through life but once. If, therefore, there be any
kindness I can show, or any good thing I can do to any fellow
being, let me do it now, for I shall not pass this way again."
-William Penn

"Men are not superior by reason of the accidents of race or color. They are superior who have the best heart- the best brain."

-Robert Ingersoll

Chapter 5
RACE

This topic really hurts my heart. It sickens me, as I'm sure it does many of you, that the issue of race still exists in America. Granted, our history definitely shows a racial divide in the past, but we should be beyond prejudice and bigotry today. We should be able to talk to and refer to others by their names, not by their color.

There is no denying our past. We all know our history, and we should treat it as such: history. Good, bad, ugly, no matter what it was, it is our history, America's history. Whatever color your skin may be, whatever your background, we all should learn from the mistakes made and celebrate the victories. The sad part is, for whatever reason, it seems we keep segregating ourselves over and over again, even after so many sacrifices have been made to bring equality for everyone.

I know we all want to be proud of our heritage, no matter what that may be, but when do we get to the point where we all recognize it as *our* heritage, *our* history? Again, it is America's history. It never ceases to amaze me that everyone, people of all color, wants racism to be behind us, but then there are clubs, TV stations, award shows, holidays, and other items and events labeled with specific skin colors. Why? What happened to the end of racism? Doesn't that kind of thing just stir up the issue of race again and help promote what we say we want to get away from?

Another thing I still hear, as I'm sure you do too, is that someone of a different skin color is holding someone else back. Please! Have you ever looked into all of the different kinds of loans, scholarships, and other programs that provide opportunities for people of specific skin colors? There are tons of them. There are all kinds of avenues of help, ranging anywhere from local, private firms all the way up to the federal level. What about this: those who work hard and have the grades or other criteria for those programs get the help, regardless of the color of their skin? Why can't it be that simple? What about applying for a job and only having your actual qualifications looked at instead of your skin color? These are just a few examples of race entering the picture when it shouldn't. When and where does it stop?

Before I go any further, let me say that I have not used any specific color of skin in my earlier examples because it really involves everyone. Every color has its own TV shows, magazines, or whatever. I just want to be clear that I am in no way referring to or suggesting anything about anybody specific because it is about all of us. Sadly, we can't just simply be Americans with red, white, and blue as the only colors we were ever concerned with.

Here is a sobering thought that should do away with what is left of racism: no matter your skin color, we have terrorists that want us all dead for simply being American. September 11, 2001 should be a constant reminder of that. I think back to that tragedy again. In the weeks and months following, we didn't have racism in America; we had nationalism. We had unity and we all need to remember that and just know it's not over.

Whatever differences we may have, we must put them aside. There is too much at stake to do otherwise, and more of us need to recognize our equality in order to keep America from continuously falling back into old ways. That does nothing but hinder and bind us, and keeps us from pulling together in other ways.

There's really not much more I know to say about this topic because I believe we should already be past it anyway, but in case you want or need to reflect a little more, I would encourage you to rediscover one of the most profound speeches ever written: "I Have a Dream" by Dr. Martin Luther King, Jr. I believe it truly sums up what America should be in regards to issues of skin color. If you allow it, I believe it will stir your heart and call your soul to a place of change and renew your faith in your fellow American regardless of the color of his skin.

Chapter 6

DEFENSE

"In the long history of the world, a few generations have been granted the role of defending freedom in its hour of maximum danger. I do not shrink from this responsibility— I welcome it. I do not believe that any of us would exchange places with any other people or any other generation. The energy, the faith, the devotion which we bring to this endeavor will light our country and all who serve it—and the glow from that fire can truly light the world.

And so, my fellow Americans: Ask not what your country can do for you—ask what you can do for your country.

My fellow citizens of the world: Ask not what America will do for you, but what together we can do for the freedom of man."

-John F. Kennedy
Inaugural Address, 1961

Peace through strength. This is a concept that seems to be a forgotten but true belief on how to keep America safe and secure. At this moment in time, arrogance and naivety are going to destroy our country, and it is up to us, the common everyday people, to stand up united and take back our government before our government takes us out.

Whether we like it or not, see it or not, want to accept it or not, we are still at war—a war in which the first shot fired was at us, and it wasn't bullets or missiles. It was airplanes: airplanes filled with our fellow citizens; airplanes filled with people on the way to see family; airplanes filled with people on business trips or vacations; airplanes filled with innocent lives taken by cowards. And of course there were the thousands of people in the Twin Towers and the Pentagon combined.

We were attacked and will be again unless we remain vigilant in taking this war back to them. How can I say that? Because the very terrorists who plotted those September attacks have openly and proudly told us they will do it again. On that day, they danced in the streets as we mourned. They burned our flag in celebration as we watched in sadness as the smoke rose up from the ashes. As they danced and laughed at murdering innocent people, we shed tears and held vigils in remembrance. Have we forgotten that? Have we become so complacent as to assume that incident was a one-time event and we should just let it go? God help us if we have.

Fortunately for us, the everyday citizens, our men and women in the military, the FBI, the CIA, and numerous other agencies have prevented many more attacks on our soil so far. There are things that go on in the defense of this nation we will never know about, and it's probably best that we don't, but just know the war is still going on.

Presently, not only do we have terrorists to worry about, we have an ever-growing tension between us and Russia and China, and their smaller partners, such as Iran, Syria, Pakistan, Egypt, and countless others. Russia and China keep building their militaries to be bigger and better. But what are we doing? In the name of politics and bureaucracy, we are cutting ours. Just in the first few months of 2012, we have learned through reports on CNN, Fox News, and many other nationwide news outlets that the Obama administration is planning to drastically decrease the size of our national defense. At a time when we have more enemies worldwide than ever before, it doesn't make sense why our government would want to make such drastic cuts to our defense system. China greatly outnumbers us when it comes to the number of total active military personnel as well as the backup manpower fit for military service. China has more backup manpower than the total population of the United States. At a time when our enemies are building up, we are tearing down. If you wanted to attack a giant, would you do it when he was standing up or would you wait until he was lying down and asleep?

There are those who say there will never be a direct attack against America by another major superpower. How foolish of you! To what extent are we willing to make that gamble? Look around with an open mind. Take a few weeks and read and watch the news. It doesn't take long to see that America is slowly being surrounded.

Russia and Iran are building missile bases in South America. We rely on China for a great deal of our manufacturing needs. What if we woke up tomorrow and the headline was that China was stopping all of its shipments to the United States immediately and indefinitely? What would we do? Most everything we have is imported from China. It's not like we could just place orders from our factories here in America. They are all in China now. What if China worked out a deal with the Middle East to purchase the oil that is generally shipped to the U.S. if the Middle East would agree to not ship it here any longer? Can't happen? Won't happen? Ask yourself, "What if?"

Say, for example, President Obama and his Cabinet do follow through with the drastic reduction of our military force and national defense. In about two years' time, our total defense force could be cut by over half. Then, imagine that the other scenario takes place with China and the Middle East. We now have our defenses cut, our supply of goods cut, and our oil cut. What would we really be able to do about it? We can't drill for oil. We have no factories. The Environmental Protection Agency (EPA), over-regulation, and over-taxation made sure of that. What could we do? America would be in total implosion mode. Sure, this may seem extreme, but look at the numbers. Look at the facts. We never imagined September 11 either.

The reason we hear for cutting our defense is economics: we can't afford it any longer. I didn't know there was a price tag on freedom. If there has ever been a time not to cut our defense, it is now. If anything, we need to make it stronger. How do we afford it, though? Well, here are a few ideas.

The first thing would be instead of sending hundreds of millions of dollars to other countries for their militaries, put it into ours. Most of the countries we send money to couldn't care less if we lived or died. If the truth be known, and sometimes it is, a lot of the money we send goes straight to the very enemy it is supposed to be protecting us from. Sometimes we openly send it straight to our enemies. Egypt is now a prime example. The Muslim Brotherhood is now in control there. They have just recently, in 2012, announced their intent to prepare for war with Israel, yet, according to a White House press release, we are sending them $800 million. I wonder how that will be spent. Probably to help follow through with their intentions to make war against Israel. Think about that. We want to send $800 million to a country that now plans to prepare to make war against Israel, our friend. I can't even begin to imagine how that makes the people of Israel feel. We are supposed to be their greatest ally and yet we are going to send money to people who want them dead. What about putting that money into our military? That would be a start. It seems we can't do that, though; it makes too much sense.

Pakistan is another example. Sure they deny it, but someone knew Bin Laden was there. Yet again, we send them millions and millions of dollars. I wonder if anyone got the hint about where their loyalty lies when we wanted the tail of our damaged helicopter back from the Bin Laden raid. If memory serves well, Pakistan was going to give China the tail. What a friend we have! We give them millions of dollars, we eradicate their land of the world's most wanted terrorist, and they threaten to give what is left of our hardware to someone else. Why do we still provide them monetary relief?

These are just two examples. If we cut this kind of junk out, we wouldn't even have to be discussing how to afford our own military and protection. Sure, some of those in Washington say there are strategic interests involved in all of this, and I'm sure that is the case at times, but my question is, whose interest? Our security or the pockets of those nations we give money to? Just from a common-sense point of view, the odds seem to be more in their favor than ours. I think our return on investment is pretty clear in these two cases. We are helping one to prepare to fight our friend and the other to keep harboring and training terrorists to fight us. Pretty good investments. All the while we are doing that for them, we are weakening our own protection at home.

Another way we can help fund our defense instead of cutting it is to abolish or scale back all less-than-useful government departments and use that money for the military. Instead of funding the EPA to help push more businesses overseas, we could cut it back and get a two-fold return. That would end foolish and senseless over-regulations and help bring businesses back to America, thus creating jobs, and some of the money spent on the EPA could go into building more planes or ships—whatever the military needed.

We could cut the Department of Education. That money could go into defense. Besides, the federal government doesn't need to try to educate our children; that is and should be in the hands of parents and local schools, not big government. According to an online Bloomberg article, in 2009 American students ranked twenty-fifth among thirty-four industrialized countries in areas of math and science.[3] If job status applies to the Department of Education as it does to each American—do a good job, keep your job; do a bad job, you're fired—wouldn't you agree *they* need to be fired?

Let's cut what we don't really need and build what we do need. We don't need big government; we do need a strong defense. Part of a strong defense is a smaller government. Big government means less freedom, extreme intrusion, and everything our Founding Fathers fought against. A smaller government puts the power back into the hands of the American people, where it was intended to be to begin with. With the power back in our hands, private citizens and businesses can do, as a nation, what America does best, and that is to create and be innovative. By putting the power back into the hands of the people and keeping it out of the hands of bureaucracy, we will have the freedom to do what made America great to begin with, and when we can do that, being able to afford our defense won't even be an issue.

Our defense shouldn't be a bargaining chip or compromising point. Without it, we wouldn't be here. The defense of this nation is non-negotiable. We have to remain strong at all costs because America has been, still is, and hopefully will remain mankind's hope for freedom. We absolutely have to find ways to not only keep what defense we have now, but improve it and make it stronger.

---

3   Hechinger, John, "U.S. Teens Lag as China Soars on International Test," Bloomberg, published December 7, 2010, accessed February 29, 2012, http://www.huffingtonpost.com/2011/07/11/state-education-rankings-_n_894528.html.

The threats against America today are just as great, if not greater, than those of World War I and II. The enemies are many. Their tactics in some ways are the same, yet different. Some of the enemies' tactics today are more subtle. In the past, military force was the biggest threat. We still have that today, but we also have the threat of ideologies and the changing and overlooking of our Constitution. We not only have to protect ourselves militarily, but socially as well. There are people who are changing and twisting our laws, and eventually it will get to the point where we will be violating new laws just by exercising our God-given rights and the rights our Constitution provides.

Speech is an example. There are laws being put into place all over the country stating if you pray, if you use the name of God, or if you speak out against the lifestyles that some may choose, you are considered to be committing a hate crime— just for speaking out. But it seems permissible for others to speak against and criticize religious beliefs and doctrines. There are places where Christians can't pray to God, but Muslims are allowed their prayer time to Allah. The last time I looked, our money states, "IN GOD WE TRUST." The last time I checked, our Pledge of Allegiance states, "One nation under God." If we allow our founding principles to be unraveled and twisted, if we allow outside beliefs and influences to change our laws so that when we practice our founding rights we are considered to be breaking the law, then we, without the firing of a single shot, have been conquered as a nation—and we cannot allow that to happen!

As I said earlier, we are at war. War doesn't always have to involve staring down the barrel of a gun. It doesn't always take dropping bombs or rushing the frontline. Sometimes war only involves the stroke of a pen. Then great damage can come from ignorantly standing still and willingly doing nothing.

Another area where it seems we're losing is our borders. On September 11, our borders should have been locked down, no questions asked. We might as well not even have a border. For some reason, our borders have been allowed to remain open. Why? I believe that's a question most Americans ask. If it's a matter of funding, here is an idea for that. Let us impose a simple flat tax, get rid of the IRS, and turn tax agents into border agents. Some studies have shown that a simple flat tax would bring in more revenue than we receive now, and at the same time, everyone would pay a lower tax rate. Everyone wins here. However, we have to get our jobs back first. Maybe if we were to have a low, flat corporate tax rate, that would help create jobs, which would bring in more revenue and help pay for our new border agents, the former tax agents. So, here is what we would have: no bureaucratic IRS, more tax revenue with a lower rate, more jobs, and a secure border. Maybe that is farfetched, but it is simple and it might just work. You can be sure, though, that it would be better than what we have now.

We all agree that the border needs to be secured. Unfortunately, though, the damage may already be done. Over the past few years, some major news outlets have reported that known terrorists have made their way across our borders and are here right now, waiting and planning to do their damage. We may not be able to stop them, but if we had some leadership in Washington with enough guts to secure our borders instead of suing individual states, trying to do so, we could keep out others wanting to do harm to us. We could also control the population of unwanted illegal aliens here in the United States, but that is a topic for another time.

I believe it speaks volumes to us as citizens when the very entity whose primary purpose is to protect its citizens doesn't do its job—and when the citizens try to protect themselves, they are sued and punished for doing so. That should tell us all something. The first thing it should tell us is that those in power need to go, and go soon. It should also tell us that we, the people, aren't in control. When the will of the people is being ignored, we have a right and an obligation to do what needs to be done and stand against a dysfunctional, out of touch, incompetent leadership and take back and protect what is ours, America.

"We admit of no government by divine right... the only legitimate right to govern is an express grant of power from the governed."
-William Henry Harrison

"The very essence of a free government consists in considering offices as public trusts, bestowed for the good of the country, and not for the benefit of an individual or a party."
-J.C. Calhoun

"When a man assumes a public trust, he should consider himself as public property."
-Thomas Jefferson

I believe there are more threats to America today than ever before: terrorism, biological warfare, cyber warfare, nuclear proliferation, economy, ideologies, and so much more. I know I didn't even scratch the surface with my few thoughts and examples, but I hope, if nothing else, you might really think about the true threats to our national security. These threats are real. Some are upon us now, and others are looming in the not-too-distant future and could easily become reality if we, the people of this nation, don't start standing up for ourselves. Make no mistake: the threats within our borders are just as many if not more. When the so-called leadership of this country puts into place policies, mandates, and laws that go against everything America stands for, which will destroy it from the inside out, you must know that our enemies on the outside won't be too far behind. If those in control lower our shields, the enemy is sure to attack.

Where America was once respected and feared, we are now laughed at and run over. Where America once stood for something, in the eyes of the world we now fall for anything. Where America once educated the world, we are now the ones being educated. Where America was once the example of what other countries could be, we are now becoming an example of what not to be.

We are in serious trouble, and we need to see it. We can overcome it, though, and I emphasize *we*. There is some time left to change our course, but not a lot. We must act now. The security and sovereignty of America is at stake. If we lose any of it now, we may never get it back. But don't take my word for it or anyone else's. You read. You watch. You listen and look around for yourself. You make the decision. Is this worth fighting for? I believe it is. I believe you do too. May

God grant us the wisdom and strength to do what needs to be done today so America will be secure for tomorrow.

"Our country! In her intercourse with foreign nations may she always be in the right; but our country, right or wrong."

-Stephen Decatur

"The world will little note, nor long remember what we say here, but it can never forget what they did here. It is for us the living, rather, to be dedicated here to the unfinished work which they who fought here have thus far so noble advanced. It is rather for us to be here dedicated to the great task remaining before us—that from these honored dead we take increased devotion to that cause for which they here gave the last full measure of devotion—that we here highly resolve that these dead shall not have died in vain- that this nation, under God, shall have a new birth of freedom- and that government of the people, by the people, for the people, shall not perish from the earth."

-Abraham Lincoln
Gettysburg Address, 1863

Chapter 7
ECONOMY

I can remember as a teenager people in school talking about their future plans ... probably the same things you remember. There were those going to college, those going into the military, some starting their own businesses, and those who were going to get a job at the factory. Back then, if one of those didn't work out, another one was probably a sure bet. It seemed jobs weren't that scarce. Just about anyone wanting a job could go down to a local warehouse or factory and get hired. It wasn't a problem. That was just a little over twenty years ago. My, how quickly times have changed.

Today, you're lucky if you even see a factory that is open. Almost every day I pass through small towns and see what used to be the lifeblood of that community boarded up and broken down. I'm sure you've seen similar scenes. They are everywhere, and not just in small towns either. This affects big cities as well. And as you really start to look, the communities resemble these old businesses; they're boarded up and broken down too. It really gets interesting when you start talking to the people who live in those communities. Sadly, when you look into the eyes of the people as they talk, you can see what most of their souls feel. They feel just like the buildings: boarded up and broken down, and, as people, often forgotten. Well, where is the help? Why not just go to the next town? Because the next town looks and feels just the same: it's boarded up, broken down, and forgotten. I encourage you, if you have not seen the new face of America, to take a drive. Really look around. It won't take long to find a place like I've described. Often, it looks like a third world country. It's not. It's *our* backyard. If you have any heart at all, you will be moved by the scene you see and any conversation you may dare to have with its residents who call it home.

Where did all of it go? Where did the jobs, businesses, and prosperity go? Overseas or south of the border, that's where, and we all know why: economics. But with cheaper labor comes cheaper quality products. How many recalls have we had on Chinese-produced items because of lead or poisons in their products? I've lost count. As far as cheap labor, if it really is cheaper to manufacture overseas, why do we have to keep paying higher and higher prices for those goods? If something doesn't change, it's not going to matter how cheap things can be made; no one in America will have a job and the means to buy those *cheaper* products will be gone. Has anyone thought about that one? Then again, that could be the whole idea.

Another problem is all of the regulations from the government. Just a thought, but maybe the government is what needs to be regulated. When a business can't afford to keep its doors open because of over-regulation, we have a serious problem. I'm not anti-government, I am anti-*big* government. If the federal bureaucracy did to itself what it has done to countless businesses and individuals, it would lock its own doors today. Nobody wants to do away with regulations altogether. We have to have clean air and water; that's just a fact. But why can't the most advanced nation in the world have clean air and water and a reasonable amount of practical regulations? It doesn't make any sense. It's probably not supposed to make sense though. It's supposed to make dollars. Follow the money, honey, right? Just think, over the years, America's industrial might has, for all practical purposes, built the majority of successful, industrious nations today. Billions of dollars have been spent by us to build and modernize other nations, often our own enemies. At one point in time, we were the only ones truly thriving and being successful at anything we attempted, be it in areas of medicine, agriculture, aerospace, or any other endeavor, but through advancements in technology and science, we have educated most of the world on how to do and be successful in those areas as well. We, at one time, were the envy of the world, and to a small degree we still are today. To some that may sound like too proud of a claim to make by an American, but I wonder, if we weren't a giant in all major playing fields, then why has America always been the one place that the rest of the world looks to for help? And why have so many other countries sent their citizens here for higher education? We have always provided help in any way we could to other countries or here on our own soil, even to non-citizens. Again, we have even provided help to our enemies in times of need.

There's nothing wrong with helping other nations with education, economics, agriculture, medicine, or anything else for that matter. That is part of what makes us great. I believe the problem is that we have now taken a backseat to many of the places we helped build up. It seems America has become stagnant. We are falling to the back of the pack. I'll remind you again that in 2009 we ranked twenty-fifth in the world in mathematics and science. Twenty-fifth! Does that not bother you? It should outrage you. We are now being educated by those who *we* educated. What about our credit ranking downgrade? The nation that once helped build the rest of the world has now basically been ranked as second rate! What about that one? How does that one make you feel? Outraged yet? Here's another one for you. According to a 2011 U.S. Food and Drug Administration special report, imports account for somewhere between 10 and 15 percent of all food products consumed in US households. Roughly 60 percent of all consumed fruits and vegetables are imported from several other countries, with some of the top contributors being Canada, Mexico, the European Union, China, Brazil, and Indonesia.[4] The next time you are in your local grocer, really look at where your food is coming from. We used to be the bread basket of the world, but not anymore. Why do we have to buy food from any place outside our borders? We shouldn't!

While in Florida last year, I thought back to my childhood and family vacations we took there. As we rode in the car, we saw nothing but citrus trees and farms for miles and miles. Last year, those once thriving, beautiful orange groves stood as overgrown and dying fields of yesteryear. My heart sank. I rode along, looking at what used to be miles of beautiful trees hanging full of bright orange and yellow fruits and wondered if this was the picture of America. Those orchards used to provide jobs, money, and food for America. Now, they provide nothing more than a haven for insects, weeds, and thistles. I'm sure you've seen similar kinds of things where

4   "Pathway to Global Product Safety and Quality," FDA, revised July 7, 2011, accessed March 7, 2012, http://www.fda.gov/downloads/AboutFDA/CentersOffices/OfficeofGlobalRegulatoryOperationsandPolicy/GlobalProductPathway/UCM262528.pdf.

you live. Have you ever asked why? Or have you become too complacent in knowing that you can go to a convenience market or grocery store and find anything and everything you want there? Do we take that for granted? I think for the most part we do. What happens if the countries we buy our food from decide to cut us off? Then what? Our farms are gone, so we can't just start growing food overnight. I'll tell you what can grow overnight, though: chaos. A complete and total collapse of this nation would ensue. It'll never happen, you think? I'm just another conspiracy theorist, you think? Maybe, hopefully, but ask yourself, "What if?" Whether you know it or not, America's survival has slowly become dependent upon the rest of the world. We need to wake up from this nightmare! We need to decide if we, as Americans, are willing to let ourselves be guided blindly down a road that will absolutely lead us to a dead end where we lose the very essence of who we are. Are you really ready for that? If you really thought about it, you'd shout no! I'm not saying we need to isolate ourselves, because we can't. However, we can be totally self-reliant and still do business with other countries. We must absolutely remain capable of standing on our own two feet, for if we can't and if we don't America is gone. When America is gone, it won't be coming back. Just think of how many countries long for that day when America is no more, and some of them wouldn't even be here if it wasn't for us. Again, wake up, America!

I've just pinpointed a few areas here. I know you can think of several more. I challenge you to go through your residence and randomly select fifteen to twenty items. See where they were made. I would bet less than 10 percent of what you look at will read "Made in USA." It's sad but likely that nothing you select will state that. I can tell you this, from a blue-collar perspective, the name you see most often stamped or sewn onto your selected items today will ultimately be the powerhouse of the world tomorrow. Think about that one for a moment. What scares me about that fact is that USA isn't found on too many items any longer. If you don't already, I encourage you to watch *World Business;* it'll all start coming together for you then. We have allowed ourselves and possibly our future to be sold out.

I know businesses are in place to make money, and no one has a problem with that. The problem is when that business and money go elsewhere. I mentioned briefly before about over-regulating businesses. It's true that the fines and fees and everything else put on businesses make it easier and cheaper to move the business elsewhere. So, here is another thought from a common man's perspective. Why not come up with a list of everything that makes a business go overseas or just south of here and then just do the opposite to bring them back? Maybe that's too simple. Maybe it's naïve. But from my point of view, it seems like it would work. We need to bring it all back home. I'm no marketing executive, but at a time like this, I would love to have a business where I could say all my items were grown or built in America and produced by Americans. That might even increase sales. What are your thoughts on that?

Well, no matter what anyone thinks, the truth is, we need jobs. How hard can that be to understand? Everywhere you turn, it's the same story: jobs, jobs, jobs! Everywhere from the poorhouse to the White House, we hear about jobs. Well, what are we doing to get our jobs back? It seems like nothing except just talking about it. We don't need any more talk. Talk is cheap, but without jobs, even that may get to be too expensive! What we need is action!

I believe one of the best and quickest plans of action for job and economic growth would be in energy independence. However, we have one side saying let's develop alternative forms of energy while the other side is saying let's just dig and drill. What about a combination of the two? Right now, we need oil, gas, and coal. We can't change overnight what we have relied on for decades. At the same time, we don't need to discredit the other. To be effective in our transition, we really need to study and develop reliable forms of alternative energy so that when we do make the transition, there aren't any unwanted surprises. Really, how hard is it to do both?

Think of how many jobs could open up right now if we started drilling our own oil and tapped into our coal and natural gas resources. Think of the economic impact it would have on not only lowering the cost of gas at the pumps, but also on lowering the cost of goods where higher costs of transport have been passed on to the consumer. Not only would jobs and the economy grow, but our national security would definitely become more solid because we would no longer be dependent upon foreign, sometimes hostile, suppliers of oil. Thousands upon thousands of jobs could be created practically overnight if we would just harvest and use our own resources. That is only one side. While we are creating jobs and economic security for the nation as a whole by becoming energy independent, we would also be creating a massive number of other jobs in the research and development of alternative sources of fuel. Everyone wins. Why is that so hard to see? We can do both at the same time, but for some reason the powers that be just won't allow it. Maybe it's just too simple. Maybe it's because it could be done for the benefit of this nation. Or maybe it's because those who have the power to do something about it have been bought out at the expense of our country. Whatever the reason, it's definitely not the right reason. I think I speak for most Americans when I say we need leadership with the courage to put America back on the right track. We certainly don't have that right now and now's when we need it the most. "Leadership, Not Lies" would be a good slogan for someone willing to courageously make some much-needed changes. That's just a thought.

Here is another thought. We all know it is increasingly harder to have a profitable business in America, whether it is a small business or a massive corporation. We all know there are a lot of laws that need to be changed in order for us to again be the economic and manufacturing giant we once were. I believe those in charge of successful businesses would rather be based here in America than elsewhere, so why can't we sit down together in our community centers and town halls and come up with a plan to make that happen? We can study and really become familiar with the current laws, learning how to work with them instead of letting them work against us and also work to permanently change the laws to better favor the American business as they once did. We can do it; it is possible. We are a nation of innovators and entrepreneurs. Just because everything may not be in our favor doesn't mean we have to pack up shop and head elsewhere. America has never given up or given in that easily before, and we shouldn't start doing that now. Had we thrown in the towel years ago, we would have never become the nation we are today.

Granted, it will take open minds and changes of the heart. We may have to come up with different ways of compensating workers, but we can do it. It just takes the will. Americans want to work. We need to work. It is not true today as it has been the past twenty years that Americans won't work for lower wages. Everybody wants to make all they can—that is part of the American Dream—and America was built through the blood, sweat, and tears of the common man. America was built by people who weren't afraid to get their hands dirty or knuckles bloodied. America was built by people who found honor and dignity in doing work that others felt was below them. America was built by people not embarrassed to sweep floors or scrub toilets. America was built by a pride and a spirit that lived within its citizens and could be found nowhere else on earth. That is how America became great and how America will become great once again.

People before us knew they were a generation that would have to sacrifice in order to protect the future prosperity and security of this nation. I believe today we are the next generation called to do the same thing. We are at a point in time that for America to be better tomorrow, we have to sacrifice today. Most of us have felt the impact from the downfall of our economy, and for all practical purposes, we are in the same place now as those during the Great Depression. Unfortunately, those in power who could help to change it don't; they choose to look the other way. They say they feel the pain too, but they don't. How could they when they hold fundraising dinners for thirty-thousand dollars a plate?

One of those plates would pay most Americans a full year's salary.

Greed is a powerful poison. It causes those who have little to want more and those who have a lot to never know what enough may be. I believe greed is what has gotten us to this point today. Greed and pride can cause even the most righteous man to sell out. We have greedily been sold out as a nation for the sake of a dollar, and the price has been our freedom.

I mentioned earlier that there was peace through strength. Strength isn't just found in military might; it also comes in the form of economic might. The old proverb is true about how the borrower is slave to the lenders. The scary thing is that one of our primary lenders is China. There's a little food for thought.

I'll sum this up by simply saying, America has the will, the strength, and the knowhow to do whatever and achieve whatever she puts her mind to. America has never backed down or taken the back seat to anybody, until now. Well, I'm tired of seeing America take the back seat. We need to be in the driver's seat. Businessman, entrepreneur, or janitor, I'm reaching out to whoever will listen, and on behalf of other Americans who feel the same way I do. Let's do what we can with what we have. Let's roll up our sleeves and work together—blue-collar, white-collar, no collar—to come up with ways in our own communities to make America operational again. We don't need the White House or the Senate or Congress to tell us how to do it; we just need them to get out of the way and let us do what we do best. It's obvious that if all of them knew half of what they claimed to know, we wouldn't be in this place to begin with.

Again, as I have said before, it is up to us. We can't and shouldn't look to Washington for all the answers. We need to look to each other and within ourselves. America is here because of the freedom of the individual. We don't need the government telling us how to live our lives. Some want you to think we do, but we really don't. That's why our founders left Europe. We can do this, America! We have to, and we have to do it now.

I leave you with another quote that I feel can apply to this situation. It is simple, but really think about it when you read it. Think about it and where you are, where you want to be, and how you will get there. This is still America, and nothing is impossible!

> *"The battle, sir, is not to the strong alone; it is*
> *to the vigilant, the active, the brave."*
>
> -Patrick Henry

Chapter 8
THINKING INDIVIDUALLY

*"Equal and exact justice to all men, of
whatever state or persuasion [...]"*

-Thomas Jefferson

From a common man's point of view, I believe a large part of our problem in America is that most people don't think for themselves anymore. It is almost as though over time, we have been brainwashed into allowing the media and the government to tell us how we need to act and what we need to believe. We allow everyone else to tell us what is best for us and how we need to think. We are losing ourselves as individuals and subsequently that most important God-given right: our freedom. Once we allow the media and the government to control our lives, then no matter what we call ourselves, America is gone. Our founders risked literally everything so we could live as free, independent people, but still live and survive together as one nation. That is why our founding documents are so precious. They provide something for us that no other documents or declarations have ever provided for their citizens in the history of mankind. That is also why we must protect them and what they stand for no matter the cost.

I believe we have forgotten how fortunate and privileged we are as a people. I believe we take for granted the privilege of being Americans. I believe this because of what I see when I look around. I see poverty in the wealthiest nation on earth. I see greed becoming the law of the land when we live in the land of plenty. I see the very beliefs this nation was founded on being spat upon and laughed at. I see the very things that made us great now being apologized for and taken away. I know you see these things too. So, I ask this: are we going to sit silently and complacently and allow our country to be taken away or are we going to dig our heels in, hold our ground, and start pushing back up the hill to reclaim our mountain? Are we going to fold or fight? America, if there has ever been a time to fight, it is now! If the silent majority would end their silence and let their voices be heard, we could change this country today. I have mentioned it before, but we are at a make-it or break-it point in this country. We cannot wait any longer to do what we need to do now.

I think back to when I was a kid. I always heard that Democrats were for the working man and Republicans were for the rich. I grew up thinking that, just as many of you did and still do. No matter what the other side said, I wouldn't believe it and most of the time wouldn't even listen. So, I and many others fell into the traditional way of thinking, which is really not thinking at all. It's the same concept as letting the media and the government think for you. You're basically just numb.

Then one day something happened. I decided to start listening to the other side just to see what was being said. Sometimes it was painful to hear that things I assumed were true turned out to be lies. But the truth will set you free. It turns out today, at our moment in history, that everything is actually opposite of what I grew up hearing. I'll give you a few examples.

The first lie I always accepted as truth was that the Republicans were all for the rich man and to heck with the commoner. Well, the more I listened and read, the more I realized that wasn't quite right. What I didn't understand was how things worked. For instance, when the subject of cutting taxes for corporations and the wealthy comes up, people claim this is favoritism for the rich. Really? Well, something the media does a good job of not explaining well is the simple fact that corporations and rich people pretty much run things. Like it or not, the common man depends on them for jobs, and the more they get taxed, the fewer jobs there are for the common man. Less tax should, and I really emphasize should, mean more jobs. So, this one example isn't favoritism; it's survival for regular people. Do you think some rich guy is going to sweat not hiring people like the common man will sweat not having a job? Not likely. That is one thing people need to be better educated on to help close the divide caused by ignorance that leads to politicians using the "class warfare" card. Let's face it; most of us aren't going to become rich. That's not negativity; it's just true. If most of us were going to be rich, we would be rich already. Furthermore, there is no shame in the rich, the poor, and those in between working together so we can all prosper and achieve bigger and better things. That is how we became great, and that is how we need to make it again. If we sat down together in our communities as business leaders and working people and communicated to each other why we see and do things the way we do, then we could eliminate the ignorance and false assumptions and do what needs to be done to put people back to work, thus putting the country back on the right path toward prosperity.

The second lie goes hand-in-hand with the first, the lie that Republicans want to hold back the common man. All you have to do to unveil the truth about this one is simply watch news channels such as CNN and MSNBC; then truly look around to see what happens in the real world. One example of how the modern Democratic Party has become the lie it spreads about the Republican Party is the bailout plan of President Obama. It has benefited no one but the rich. Presently, who has the Senate? The Democrats. Who had both House and Senate at the time of President Obama's inauguration? The Democrats. The Republican Party currently has the House but is in a hindered position because of their level in the governmental hierarchy. For three years, though, the Democratic Party held all positions, and what did they do to bring jobs back to America? Nothing and here are a few examples showing just that.

The first big rejection for job creation from the current Democrats was refusing to build the new oil pipeline from Canada. That was handed to us, but turned down. How many thousands of jobs could we have had, but don't because of that? What about all of the jobs we could have in the drilling, refining, and transportation of oil and gas? What about the economic and security impact that could have for us? That is another "No!" for the American people from the Democratic Party. What about the cuts in defense? How many soldiers will lose their jobs? What about the companies who supply the military? Less supplies means less jobs. Less military means less national security. Again, we can thank the current Democratic Party for that. What about all of the green jobs promised? The last I heard was that most of those billions of dollars given by us, to create jobs for us, are gone just like companies they were given to. One example is Solyndra. Know that name? That was the green energy solar-panel company that was given $500 million of taxpayer money to create jobs and then went bankrupt! What about all of the shovel-ready jobs? I wonder if anyone thought that these few jobs created would only be temporary. Sooner or later, whatever is being constructed will be complete. If nothing else is shovel-ready, then those jobs are gone. Who does the proud, hard-working, blue-collar man have to thank for that one? The Democratic Party, that's who.

What about all of the promises for the housing market? The year 2011 had the worst home sales record in decades, maybe ever. That's a real boost for jobs, not to mention morale. The list goes on and on and on. Sure, everyone wants to pass the buck back to President Bush, but, in case someone forgot, for almost three full years the Democratic Party had full control of everything, and what happened? Are you better off today than four years ago? If so, good for you, but I have a strong feeling most of you said no.

So, with all of that, I come back to thinking for ourselves. How much more is it going to take for us to stop thinking what we're told to think and start believing what we know the truth to be? I'm not trying to persuade anyone to go to one political party or the other; all I'm trying to say is that no matter what you have been told, start listening to both sides, research and look at the facts, and then make up your own mind. But you have to have an open mind and heart to arrive at a conclusion you believe is the truth. Maybe you like where we are as a nation. I certainly hope not, because it would truly concern me as your fellow American if you were content with how things are right now considering we have record-high unemployment levels and a failing education system and we are at risk of having our very freedom of speech stripped away.

We are heading in the exact opposite direction of where our founders began. They demanded truth; we accept lies. They demanded independence; we accept intrusion. They believed in hard work; today, a lot of people believe in hardly working. They provided small government and liberty; we accept big government and tyranny. They believed in God-given rights; today, we reject God and expect special rights. They believed in sovereignty; we believe in selling out. They believed in the sanctity of life; we believe in taking life for convenience. What more needs to be said? Don't take my word for it; all you have to do is look around and you'll see for yourself.

America is a ship that must be turned around. We can hear the waterfall in the distance, and there is only so much time before the current is too strong to change course. Old, young, rich, or poor, we are America, and we have to turn around now! So, I ask you this: if you love this country and want it to be here for future generations, what will you do today to help preserve it and make it better for tomorrow? Think for yourself.

> *"The God who gave us life, gave us*
> *liberty at the same time."*
>
> -Thomas Jefferson

> *"Liberty and Union, now and forever,*
> *one and inseparable."*
>
> -Daniel Webster

Chapter 9
CHOICES

"You are free the moment you do not look outside yourself for someone to solve your problems."

-Anonymous

I would like to go back to something I mentioned earlier about how being an American is a privilege, not a right. I know people look at this in different ways; quite often we are trying to say the same thing, but depending upon the words we use, it may come across differently, creating senseless arguments and disagreements. So, I am going to try to clarify my view a little better and paint a bigger picture.

I do believe being an American, whether by birth or legal immigration, is an honor and a privilege. Because of that, we should live in a way that upholds what our founding beliefs stand for. I do not believe being an American is a right. I say that because none of us get to choose where we are born. If we are born in the United States, I believe it is truly by the grace of God that He allowed us to be here. Now, by being born here, we do have a birthright to this nation, which in turn gives us all of the rights afforded us in our Constitution. Should a person be born elsewhere and want to live here that person has a right to pursue citizenship here. Once that is acquired, then that person is entitled to the same rights as a natural-born citizen. The unique thing about our American Constitution is that it has been the only document in the history of man that gives and protects the very rights God gave man to begin with. Recognizing where true freedom begins is one attribute that helped to make America great.

As citizens of this great nation, we all have the right to pursue whatever goals or dreams our hearts desire. We have the ability, if we choose, to become what we want to become and do what we want to do. No matter how big or how small our aspirations are, our Constitution gives us that liberty. That is our right.

However, it seems that as time has gone on, a lot of people have bought into the lie that they have a right to demand from the government a free ride. They believe they have a right to do nothing and get paid for it. Well, they are only half right. They can choose to be lazy and non-productive, that is their right, but the hard-working, tax-paying people who contribute to society have the right to tell them no. Our tax dollars will no longer pay for the upkeep of society's slothful by choice. The key word here is *choice*. Being the nation we are, we should help our fellow citizens who truly need help and can't provide for themselves; as a matter of fact, it is our duty to help the helpless, but we shouldn't feel obligated or be forced to aid those who have chosen a non-productive lifestyle.

"Success comes before work only in the dictionary."

-Anonymous

Choice is what I want to bring attention to. Somewhere along the line we, as a nation, have stopped teaching responsibility and self-respect and started teaching and accepting the notion that we need to depend on the government. We have traded hard work and dignity for laziness and a lack of self-worth. This goes against everything our founders believed as well as everything we should believe. The programs put in place years ago that were supposed to be the beginning of a new life have become a way of life. Our system has failed in helping to get people off of welfare and back to work. It has failed in giving people real hope and dignity. The system has made people become reliant on the government instead of being self-reliant and free from the government. Unfortunately, with our economy down right now, it will take a while to fix this even if we really wanted to. That brings me to the following questions. Do we really want to fix things? Do we really want people to be productive or are we just giving a lot of lip service to this and other issues in order to sound like we care when really we don't?

I believe we do care, but what can we do about it? The first thing we can do is to get elected officials in office, from the local level to the White House, who will really care and put the people first instead of their own self-interests. That is another great thing about America: we are one of the few nations on earth where we can change our leadership without having to implement riots and chaos. With order and peace, we can change the course of this nation by simply voting. But we have to do it.

The second thing we can do is to start teaching people about self-worth again. We need to start reeducating people that we can be whatever we want to be if we just try. Sadly, the norm has become to blame everyone and everything else for our lot in life instead of taking responsibility for our own decisions and actions. We need to start teaching that simple, scientific truth that applies to more than just science: for every action there is an equal and opposite reaction. If one chooses to drop out of high school and not get a diploma or GED, life will be a lot harder. Everything from getting a job to joining the military becomes far more difficult. But we just blame society. People start using drugs and alcohol, and when they develop a problem and become dependent, what do we say? "Well, they had an awful childhood." People get pregnant and have children they don't want or want to be responsible for.

Then all we hear is how it was the fault of the other person in the relationship: "He made me do it," or "She wasn't on the pill." Then you have people who blame America as a whole for their grief in life. They say America's arrogance has oppressed them or capitalism has deprived them. To those people I'd ask, "Why are you still here?" Maybe it's because America hasn't been that bad to them. It could be that some of them have made their riches off of stirring up fear and hatred in others, making others believe they are oppressed, thus making themselves feel important. No matter what the situation is, it seems it's always somebody else's fault. In some cases, that may indeed be true, but ultimately we make our own choices, we choose our own paths. It is time that individuals start taking responsibility for their own actions.

Choices go the other way also. Good choices lead to good results. Hard work can still pay off. I know it seems less and less like this, but we can't have achievements unless we try, and we won't try if we continuously blame others. If one thing doesn't work, try to do something else. If the people around you are a negative influence, do your best to be around people who are a positive influence. As the old saying goes, "You can't soar like an eagle if you fly with turkeys."

This is another one of those things that we have to get right in our own hearts and minds first before we can expect things around us to change. Granted, electing new leadership and changing laws and programs is a start, but we really need to begin with ourselves first. Then, once we get our hearts right, we can associate with other like-minded individuals and eventually change things in our communities to help restore America's original purpose: to provide the safety, security, and freedom for every individual to have life, liberty, and the pursuit of happiness. Those are our rights. They are our God-given rights, and unless we can change this mindset of blame and unworthiness, those God-given rights are in jeopardy of being taken away by a handful of individuals who lust for power and gamble our liberty and self-integrity in exchange for individual dependency on the government.

There are those in power at the local level and all the way up to the top who want us to believe they know what is best for us. They want us to believe we need government to run our businesses and finances. They want us to believe our Constitution is a thing of the past and our laws and court decisions need to incorporate European and Islamic laws. There are people in power who even want to tell us we can't eat a cheeseburger and fries if we want to, for crying out loud!

Well, guess what? They don't know what is best for us. They don't know how to run our businesses and finances. If they did, we wouldn't have record unemployment levels, the lowest records of home sales, a record number of businesses going bust, a military being dismantled, and the highest number of people on food stamps in history. The federal government shouldn't be involved in trying to run the private sector to begin with. They need to leave it alone and let the private sector do what it does best and build America. As far as our judges making court rulings with the aid of foreign law, they need to be kicked off the bench and sent elsewhere to live under those foreign laws. I don't remember "We, the people" giving authority for us to be ruled outside of our Constitution. Last but not least, if we want to eat cheeseburgers, we can eat

cheeseburgers. That is also our right. I strongly encourage
you to research the topics mentioned above on your own, and
when you do, you'll discover for yourself that the picture of
America and our future is grim.

In spite of all the negative, there is still a silver lining,
and if I don't get any other point across in this book, I hope
this one gets through: this is still America. We, the people,
still have the Constitution. It is there for us. We are still the
voice. If the people we send to our congressional and Senate
seats don't do the job we sent them there to do, let's fire them!
That is our right!

Many of you are probably now like I used to be: taking
what I had heard my entire life for granted as being the truth.
I would listen to the mainstream news and just accept things
as they were presented. In doing so, I was at times accepting
lies. It wasn't until I made myself listen to both sides—and
I mean really listen—that I started realizing the truth about
a lot of things. I had to open my mind and my heart. That
is hard for a lot of us to do, but until we do, nothing will
change.

I'm going to list some people I would encourage you to
really listen to. Their styles are different. Their presentations
are different. You may not agree with everything they say,
and some will rub you the wrong way. However, if you don't
listen to them already, give it a try. You'll have to give it some
time, but please do; I promise it will be worth it. Here you go:
Sean Hannity, Glenn Beck, Rush Limbaugh, Bill O'Reilly,
Mike Huckabee, Michael Barry, Jay Sekulow and the ACLJ
(American Center for Law and Justice), Mark Levin, Phil

Valentine, Ralph Bristol, Steve Gill, Michael DelGiorno, Chris Plante, and G. Gordon Liddy.

Whether you like, believe, or agree with any of these people or not, the one thing you should like, believe, and agree with is they are all fighting to preserve our rights and our liberty. When you listen to both sides and understand that America is about real freedom, it won't take long to see who is really fighting for America and who is fighting to destroy it and ultimately you and me, since *we* are America. America is our families and our futures. America is our dreams. What side will you choose? If you love your rights and freedom, then you will choose wisely. If you won't think for yourself, you'll fall for anything and you will choose foolishly. There is a choice to be made if America is to survive.

In thinking about this and other things I included earlier, one way we might be able to reinstitute an appreciation for self-worth and national pride is to promote people joining the military. Instead of dismantling our military, why don't we cut out the ways we waste funds and use that money to promote our armed forces? Think about it. Right now, with the economy down, a lot of people, including younger men and women, can't find work, so let's grow the military with those younger folks. We would take money being wasted, such as the *aid* to Pakistan, and put it to good use. We would be building our national defense all the while putting people to work. With more people joining the military, we would need more supplies. That should mean opening our factories and creating jobs to manufacture those supplies for our men and women in uniform. Not only would the men and women volunteering for military duty come to have a new love and respect for America, but those people in our factories would have a renewed sense of pride in America by being able to build top-quality, American-made products for our national defense. It may sound crazy to some, but it makes sense to me. Isn't that how we used to do it, anyway? It worked then; it could work again because this is still America and we can accomplish anything we set our minds to!

> *"Our thoughts determine our responses to life. We are not victims of the world. To the extent that we control our thoughts, we control the world."*
>
> -Anonymous

> *"But Jesus beheld them, and said unto them, 'With men this is impossible; but with God all things are possible.'"*
>
> -Matthew 19:26 KJV

Chapter 10
CHANGE AND THE AMERICAN GOOD

I know most of what I have included in this book has been common issues and challenges that we are all aware of and face as a nation. There will always be challenges we have to confront and overcome, and everyone will always have different opinions on how to do just that. As we all know, the hard part is learning how to listen, compromise, and agree on the solutions to those challenges.

There are some things I have repeated myself on. The reason I have done that is to emphasize the importance of things we need to remember and take seriously as Americans. Most of what I have written about is not just my thoughts and opinions, but also the thoughts and opinions of people I have spoken with over many years of interacting with the public. I am fortunate in my line of work to have the ability to learn from the life experiences of other people who are willing to share their thoughts and knowledge with me. I find that most people are concerned about the same things as everyone else and that certainly includes the future of America. Everyone, young and old, rich and poor, shares a lot of the same thoughts and feelings about what is happening in our country.

I've just barely scratched the surface with this book and the topics I've chosen to include within it. I know if you have read through to this point, you have probably had more thoughts and feelings than you imagined you would. I hope that's the case, because that has been my one intention with the completion of this project. My views could have been more profound and included many more details, but I really wanted to keep things as simple and direct as possible. Quite often, simple and direct is the best approach; even when challenges seem so complex, the best answers are sometimes the simplest. I have written this to be a reminder that our challenges right now are many, but also for it to be a direct awakening to the fact that we have the fortitude to meet those challenges head-on, overcome each one, and make America the best it has ever been.

So many of us believe we can't do anything, but we can! As a matter of fact, change begins with each of us, the individuals. We can't expect everything around us to change if we don't change ourselves. As I pointed out earlier, when each of us changes on a personal level, then our communities change for the better, and then our country can change. That's how it works; it's a chain reaction that starts with us.

"What kind of change?" you ask. Well, let's look at that here. The hardest change is within our hearts. When bad things happen in our lives again and again, we have a tendency to allow our hearts to become cold and hard. At that point, no matter what anyone else tries to do to help us, only we have the ability to change ourselves—and we can only change our hearts when we really want to. Until then, we shut down and close ourselves off, becoming bitter and selfish and wanting to blame everyone else for our problems. Or we become stuck, blaming ourselves for our problems, but not feeling worthy enough to forgive ourselves, learn from our mistakes, and move on with our lives. Again, we have to first become the change we want to see in others before anything else can change. That means digging deep, swallowing pride, and doing whatever it takes to overcome our prejudices, hatred, distrust, or whatever else is in the way. But it can be done. That is the kind of change I am referring to. Hopefully, if you are looking for something positive, the direction I am going now will help.

In spite of all of our challenges and issues, America is still a nation full of good things and good people. Think about when disaster strikes. That may seem like a contradiction since disasters are never good, but it is a fact that America shines in the aftermath of disaster. It is a testimony to the American spirit when you watch the news coverage of floods, tornadoes, and other disasters and see people helping in any way they can. It's stranger helping stranger, with no motive in mind except to help someone else in need. People come from all over the country to the places where disaster strikes, bringing with them whatever resources they have, often just themselves, to help piece back together the lives of their fellow Americans. Some of the most moving stories are those in which a family has lost their home and all their belongings, but instead of dealing with their own loss, they are down the street helping a neighbor. We see people in boats risking life and limb to rescue pets and people who are stranded on rooftops or in trees after a flood. We see people providing the basic needs of others by handing out food, water, and blankets. Sometimes we even see teddy bears being given to children who are scared and don't understand what's happened. A small, furry friend can provide the basic need of a child to feel safe and secure. The examples could go on and on, but the one thing that stands out to me most about all of it is that it isn't the government or any one organization doing everything. It always begins with the people. Sure, the government helps, and organizations, such as the Red Cross, step in, but it starts with your average, everyday people.

Why? Because the majority of people in America care about their fellow man.

That being said, if we truly do care about our fellow man, especially when there's trouble, we need to start allowing our voices to be heard instead of allowing a handful of people to act as stumbling blocks for the progression and freedom of the rest of us. The majority of Americans want to do what is right and get this country back on the path it should be on, but for some reason we're not doing that. Why not? Because the majority of Americans feel powerless when they shouldn't. The power is actually in our hands, and it is time for the sleeping giant to wake up.

Another great thing we see happen in America whenever disaster strikes is the utilization of some of the greatest talent in the world. No matter what side of the aisle they are on, entertainers of all kinds come together for benefits to raise money whenever the need arises. Children collect change and aluminum cans for money to help as part of church or school projects. However, it doesn't always take disaster to unite us.

Every day, all over the country, people carry food to those who are shut in and can't get out. People volunteer in local soup kitchens to feed others who are homeless and hungry. Different clubs and private organizations hold auctions to raise money for injured firemen and police officers or for their families if they have perished in the line of duty. Friends and families hold car washes or concerts to help loved ones pay for medical expenses after surgeries or cancer treatments. In spite of all that is negative in America there are still those unsung, everyday, common people who try to find ways to help their fellow Americans who really are in need. It's wonderful that those people take responsibility for helping others in need, but that responsibility really belongs to all of us. Imagine what it would be like if no one cared enough to help someone else besides himself; now imagine how great this country could be if *everyone* gave a helping hand.

By the grace of God, we are the most blessed nation in all of existence. Not only is the spirit that lives in us driven to pursue a better way of life for us and our families, but the American spirit also strives in the pursuit of making life better for all who thirst for the American dream. Even though selfishness, egotism, and greed are all human characteristics, as Americans, we are called to be better than that and to rise above those traits. Our Founding Fathers were able to do so, and the proof of their success is revealed in our Declaration and Constitution. Some may say they're only words, but those words have given all of us and the world around us hope. The seriousness of our documents should not be taken lightly.

No matter how sophisticated and advanced we become, at the core of everything is still basic humanity, and we must never forget that. We must never forget that there is always good and evil, and sometimes evil will arrive in sheep's clothing. However, with open minds and pure hearts, America will always overcome evil with good. As long as we hold true to the course our founders laid, we will always be the hope and light in a dark world. As long as we hold true to the faith our Founding Fathers had in the one true God, our hearts will never fail and our feet will never stumble. We will stay the course.

"The God who gave us life, gave us liberty at the same time."

-Thomas Jefferson

What do you see that is good in America? Many choose to see nothing. Many who live here choose to do nothing but curse America and teach hatred against America. The one thing those people often fail to acknowledge is that even though they speak against America, it is America that gives them that right, the right to freedom of speech. There are parts of the world where if you just simply speak against the governing body, you will be put to death. We see it in the news all of the time. Maybe that is why those hate-filled people remain here; they'd rather live here and hate it, but be free at the same time, than go elsewhere and be forced to remain silent. Even the haters of America still find something good in it.

So I come back to you, the reader, and ask, what do you see or find good in America? Hopefully you can think of a lot of ways to answer that question, because there really are a lot of good things to celebrate here. Let not your heart be troubled, because the bell of liberty still rings for you. Whatever you find good and wherever you want this dream called America to take you, I leave you with the following quotes.

"Ideals are like stars; you will not succeed in touching them with your hands. But like the seafaring man on the desert of waters, you choose them as your guides, and following them you will reach your destiny."

-Carl Schurz

"You see things that are and say, 'Why?' But I dream things that never were and say, 'Why not?'"

-George Bernard Shaw

Summary

A NEW DAY FOR AMERICA

I'm sure various things I have included in this book will be interpreted by some people as pessimistic; however, there is a difference between stating facts, as I have tried to do, and having a negative outlook. No matter what political party you side with or religious beliefs you hold, there is one fact that is indisputable and unfortunate: America's very survival is at stake. Some may say that is just one man's opinion, but when you look at our history and our past place in the world compared to today, there is no mistake that the survival of America as we know it hinges on the next few years. There are major decisions that have to be made, and they need to be made by serious people who love this country and understand what America is truly about. The decisions that need to be made should not fall to those who only live in the politics of the here and now, but to those who see the promise of a better America for tomorrow. It is up to us, the people, to elect leaders who aren't worried about political consequences, but will do what needs to be done to secure that promise.

I believe in America. I believe we, her people, have a raw determination and an unbridled spirit that can be matched by no one. We have the freedom to dream and turn dreams into reality. We have the will and ability to make America what it once was and what it should always be: a light in the darkness, the city on a hill. America should always be a true beacon of hope for the hopeless, strength to the weary, and the fountain of freedom for all who truly thirst for our God-given rights as people. Let us not just quietly idle above the treetops when we have the spirited ability to soar above the clouds; it's time for us to climb aboard and soar, America!

We all have enjoyed the security and liberty provided for us by earlier generations. But what are we providing for the future generations? That is the question we must answer. Will they be able to look back and thank us for what we have done today? Or will they curse us for things we should have done to give them the country that was given to us? If there has ever been a time we need to stand together, it is now. Let us first do in our communities what needs to be done today so we can do as a country what needs to be done tomorrow.

"Democracy is two wolves and a lamb voting on what to have for lunch. Liberty is a well-armed lamb contesting the vote."

-Benjamin Franklin

There is a social phenomenon known as the *bystander effect*, a psychological theory that people are less likely to help in emergency situations when others are observing. People are less likely to intervene when a greater number of bystanders are present, and more likely to help when few or no other people are around. The explanation for this occurrence is that people feel less responsible to help when others are available to. This is called diffusion of responsibility. Also, people take social cues from others around them, meaning they basically follow suit. If others aren't helping, then the need must not be that great or socially acceptable, so the need for help is unfulfilled.[5] This theory typically applies to emergency situations, but I believe it could easily apply to the present

---

5   Cherry, Kendra, "The Bystander Effect: What is the Bystander Effect?" About.com Psychology, accessed July 2, 2012, http://psychology.about.com/od/socialpsychology/a/bystandereffect.htm.

state of America. We can't sit back and just wait for someone else to take responsibility for helping this nation. If everyone does that nothing will ever change and things won't get any better. Each of us must step up and become a leader for this country and take responsibility for it. It is absolutely essential for America to survive.

Whatever your lot in life, know that thousands upon thousands of people have died to give you, me, and everyone else the freedom to choose if we want to pursue bigger and better things in life or just accept where we are right now. It is our choice. I know what I choose; what about you?

My fellow Americans, hold fast to what we have here and never let go. This is a vital time for us, and if we cherish what we have in America and want to pass it on to our children and our children's children, we will get serious about our times. I hope something you have read may have ignited a spark or rekindled an old one to help you do what you need to do to make our country a better one. Whether it was my words or the words of history on the pages of this book, I hope you have been inspired and come to a better appreciation of this gift we have called America. It is ours. We have no excuses. It is paramount that we leave it a better and brighter place than it was when we got here. Thank you again. God bless you, and God bless America!

> *"Do not pray for easy lives. Pray to be stronger men! Do not pray for tasks equal to your powers. Pray for powers equal to your tasks."*
>
> -Philip Brooks

Look closely at the cover of this book and the position of the sun. What do *you* see? Is light beginning to break or is darkness closing in? Is it the dawning of a new day for us as Americans or is the sun setting on the great nation we once knew?

> "*Do not go gentle into that good night.*
> *Rage, rage against the dying of the light.*"
>
> -Dylan Thomas

Cherry, Kendra. "The Bystander Effect: What is the Bystander Effect?" *About.com Psychology.* Accessed July 2, 2012. http://psychology.about.com/od/socialpsychology/a/bystandereffect.htm.

Department of Defense. "Demographics 2010 Profile of the Military Community." *MilitaryHOME FRONT.* Accessed March 4, 2012. http://www.militaryhomefront.dod.mil//12038/Project%20Documents/MilitaryHOMEFRONT/Reports/2010_Demographics_Report.pdf.

Hechinger, John. "U.S. Teens Lag as China Soars on International Test." *Bloomberg.* Published December 7, 2010. Accessed February 29, 2012. http://www.huffingtonpost.com/2011/07/11/state-education-rankings-_n_894528.html.

US Food and Drug Administration. "Pathway to Global Product Safety and Quality." *FDA.* Revised July 7, 2011. Accessed March 7, 2012. http://www.fda.gov/downloads/AboutFDA/CenterOffices/OfficeofGlobalRegulatoryOperationsandPolicy/GlobalProductPathway/UCM262528.pdf.